People Analytics Explained

Publisher's note
Every possible effort has been made to ensure that the information contained in this book is accurate at the time of going to press, and the publishers and authors cannot accept responsibility for any errors or omissions, however caused. No responsibility for loss or damage occasioned to any person acting, or refraining from action, as a result of the material in this publication can be accepted by the editor, the publisher or the author.

First published in Great Britain and the United States in 2025 by Kogan Page Limited

Kogan Page
Kogan Page Ltd, 2nd Floor, 45 Gee Street, London EC1V 3RS, United Kingdom
Kogan Page Inc, 8 W 38th Street, Suite 902, New York, NY 10018, USA
www.koganpage.com

EU Representative (GPSR)
Authorised Rep Compliance Ltd, Ground Floor, 71 Baggot Street Lower, Dublin D02 P593, Ireland
www.arccompliance.com

Kogan Page books are printed on paper from sustainable forests.

© Kogan Page, 2025

ISBNs
Hardback   978 1 3986 2441 2
Paperback   978 1 3986 2442 9
Ebook   978 1 3986 2443 6

British Library Cataloguing-in-Publication Data
A CIP record for this book is available from the British Library.

Typeset by Hong Kong FIVE Workshop, Hong Kong
Printed and bound by CPI Group (UK) Ltd, Croydon CR0 4YY

To Dhru, my cornerstone.

To Xiaorong, who taught me that being roughly right is better than being precisely wrong.

To the people analytics community, who continue to inspire and open doors for new talent.

Contents

Introduction

Introducing people analytics

So, you have decided to explore the fascinating world of people analytics. Congratulations! This book has been written for those embarking on or at the early stages of a career in the field. You might be transitioning from a different field, such as human resources (HR) or business analysis, you might have just completed a related under- or postgraduate course, or you might be starting out as a data analyst within a People team. No matter what route you've taken into your first role in people analytics, this book is for you.

People analytics is a fascinating field to delve into, and you might be drawn to it for various reasons. Human behaviour within organizational settings is complex. People analytics can impose order over chaos by simplifying complex issues into clear, actionable insights to empower leaders to make better decisions. It can improve employee experiences and culture. It can do good by measuring the intangibles to give voices to the people who are not enabled to have one. Commercially, it can make sure the right business problems are solved to reduce waste in resources and talent.

We are facing a time of unprecedented change within workplaces, with emerging trends such as artificial intelligence (AI) and autonomous systems, which is likely to have a revolutionary impact on the people analytics profession through changing organizational dynamics.[1] Our current modes of learning may not be agile enough to build professionals able to adapt as fast as technology evolves. This book seeks to equip the next generation of people analytics professionals with essential skills to enable them to navigate this changing landscape. People tend to be biased towards the importance of technical skills, but technical skills are not everything that will help you build agility to deal with changes in the long term.

Opportunities in people analytics are plentiful and growing. The barrier to 'breaking into' and succeeding in the field isn't a lack of openings, it is a lack of essential yet rarely taught skills. This book is crafted precisely to address those gaps. It emphasizes informal, foundational skills such as systems thinking, relationship management, and practical project and change management strategies that can empower you to confidently enter and excel in people analytics.

Why this book is different

As this book takes a different approach to teaching people analytics, it is likely to differ from typical technical manuals you might be familiar with. Let's begin by clarifying what to expect to ensure the book meets your expectations and supports your learning journey. You might feel it's somewhat 'high-level' compared with technical resources that teach specific coding skills or analysis methods (for instance, how to perform a regression analysis in Python or R). Equally, if you have encountered consulting-oriented people analytics texts, you may find this book more 'technical' by comparison. This is intentional. The purpose is not simply to add yet another layer of technical complexity or replicate consulting case studies, but rather to equip you with a strategic, architectural understanding of people analytics as a field.

The reality is that thriving in people analytics requires more than technical expertise or consulting skills. Before you can fully benefit from those specialist resources in the market, you need foundational knowledge – a comprehensive view of the profession, its elements, who its neighbours are in the environment and how its many elements interact. You need to understand what tools or methods to use at what time. No book can contain everything you'll ever need to do your job well, but this book aims to include the essential concepts, frameworks and keywords that will allow you to deepen your learning, specialize and flourish in your career.

The structure of this book

We begin in Chapter 1 by defining people analytics, exploring its evolution and scope, and critically assessing current trends that often overly focus on technical skills. We discuss why effective people analytics involves balancing relationship building and technical insights.

Chapter 2 gives you the tools to set yourself apart from those who don't read this book. We introduce the concept of branding in people analytics and explain how systems thinking provides a powerful framework for building your professional brand. You will gain a practical understanding of what systems thinking is and how branding and systems thinking complement each other, allowing you to position yourself strategically within the profession.

Chapter 3 dives deeply into relationship-building skills – crucial yet frequently overlooked skills in business and particularly critical in people analytics. It includes real-world practitioner stories, practical tools for understanding stakeholders, methods for mapping organizational dynamics, and strategies for establishing trust.

We then move on to the essential skill of project management, including various methodologies and approaches. Chapter 4 explains how to navigate common challenges specific to managing people analytics projects, helping you become more effective and confident in this element of the job.

Change management is central to making analytics insights actionable. In Chapter 5, we cover why change management matters and explain detailed processes for doing it as well as how to customize approaches, tools and methodologies to effectively guide organizations through transitions.

Chapters 6 and 7 synthesize everything into practical frameworks, highlighting the intersection between consulting, data analysis and data storytelling. This integration will empower you to clearly communicate insights and drive meaningful organizational decisions.

Our final chapter, Chapter 8, provides the essential business context to help you feel more confident in a people analytics role.

Last but not least, the book's Conclusion focuses on the future of people analytics, the emerging trends that will impact early career professionals today.

Throughout the book, you will find reflection points, tips and exercises to deepen your learning and set the discussion in your unique organizational context. Each chapter also ends with review questions to test your learning and understanding, as well as further reading suggestions. Use the endnotes to discover more about any research, reports or publications from other organizations discussed throughout.

Some exercises are called 'What would you do?'. These ask you to reflect on what you would do in specific scenarios, often related to fictional case studies. There are not necessarily any 'right' answers to these exercises. Think about what you would do in these scenarios, using the content in the chapter when necessary to determine your answer. After you have had a chance to reflect, you can then visit the Appendix, where you will find suggested answers.

By reading this book, the field of people analytics will no longer appear mysterious or intimidating. Instead, you will clearly see its essential elements and how everything comes together, feel empowered with practical tools, and confidently chart your path to success. *You* are the future of people analytics. So, are you ready to embark on your people analytics journey?

Let's begin.

Endnote

1   Polzer, J T (2022) The Rise of People Analytics and the Future of Organizational Research, *Research in Organizational Behavior*, www.sciencedirect.com/science/article/pii/S0191308523000011 (archived at https://perma.cc/YR8V-L452)

CHAPTER ONE

Is people analytics what you think it is?

Introduction

People analytics (PA) is one of the most sought-after capabilities in modern workplaces. But do you know what it entails, exactly? In this chapter, we explore the foundations of PA, beginning with a clear definition of the term, its related fields and role in the organization. We then take a look at how the function is typically organized within companies, before briefly considering the history of PA.

We explore how the function has grown in prominence, as well as in scope, and how the conversation has often skewed heavily towards technical skills, which then segways into the integrated approach of this book, focusing on relationship building.

By the end of this chapter, you'll have a clearer understanding of what PA is (and isn't), why it matters and a new way of thinking about the attainment of PA skills.

LEARNING OBJECTIVES

By the end of this chapter, you will be able to:

- Articulate what PA is and why it plays a critical role in both HR and broader business strategy.
- Describe the historical development of PA.
- Explain how PA extends beyond data analysis to include behavioural insights, stakeholder alignment, and organizational impact.
- Discuss the benefits and limitations of current PA trends, including the heavy focus on technical skills and tools.
- Reflect on and challenge common assumptions about what PA is, and what it isn't in today's workplace.

Defining PA and its role

People love labels. They help us remember complex ideas, but they also create unnecessary debates, especially in the world of HR and analytics. The reality? PA terms are often used interchangeably, and can mean slightly different things to different people or organizations. Still, each has its own 'typical' definition. We'll start by looking at some of these definitions and their differences, but remember that the key isn't terminology, it's how data helps make better decisions.

When people refer to 'people analytics', they typically mean the efforts of using people data to generate value. This goes beyond HR data and requires a more systematic approach to viewing problems. Sometimes, PA is often referred to as 'workforce analytics' or 'talent analytics'.

HR analytics is about using data to improve HR and aid its decision-making. It focuses on traditional HR functions, such as recruitment, learning and development and diversity, equity and inclusion (DEI).

HR reporting is the fundamental element of HR analytics and PA. It involves collecting and organizing data to create metrics, such as headcount, turnover rates and absenteeism, as well as reports.

A useful way to organize (but not strictly define) these terms is through an analytics maturity model, illustrating how organizations grow in their use of workforce data. This typically includes four stages:[1]

- Descriptive: Understanding what happened.
- Diagnostic: Exploring why things happened.
- Predictive: Anticipating future outcomes.
- Prescriptive: Recommending actions to optimize results.

At the most fundamental level, HR reporting is primarily descriptive, giving a snapshot of past events. It's more about 'what happened' than 'why it happened' and offers little interpretation or predictive insight.

Moving up in maturity, HR analytics expands beyond reporting to include diagnostic analytics ('Why did it happen?'), analysing trends and relationships to uncover the root causes of HR challenges. This may include investigating why turnover is rising in a certain department or what factors influence employee engagement.

Further along the maturity curve, PA takes a broader, more strategic approach, encompassing predictive and prescriptive analytics ('What will happen?' and 'What should we do?'). It connects workforce data to business outcomes, forecasting trends like future leadership potential or attrition risks, and providing data-driven recommendations to guide talent.

People analytics: A systematic approach to using people data to generate value. Sometimes referred to as 'workforce analytics' or 'talent analytics'.

HR analytics: Using data to improve HR functions such as recruitment, learning and development and DEI.

HR reporting: The process of collecting and organizing HR data into metrics such as turnover and headcount and reporting on them.

STOP AND THINK

Consider a recent example of someone talking about PA in your organization. What did they really mean – PA, HR analytics or HR reporting? Was it clear what they meant at the time, or did you spot any confusion?

PA's nearest neighbours

In this section, we'll consider fields that are very close to PA. In some organizations, they may be part of the PA organizational structure, while in others, they may be completely separate.

WORKFORCE PLANNING

Workforce planning (WFP) is complex and requires collaboration across HR, Finance and Operations, which often have conflicted priorities – a key reason why many organizations struggle to get it right.

It has two common types:

1 Strategic workforce planning (SWP)[2]: Typically sits in HR, Finance, or Strategy, focusing on long-term talent needs, workforce trends, and predictive modelling.
2 Operational workforce planning (OWP): Usually managed by Operations, ensuring the right staffing levels in the short term to meet immediate business demands.

Because WFP requires inputs and synergies from multiple functions, true success comes from breaking silos – aligning talent insights, cost planning and real-time workforce deployment for a competitive edge.

TALENT INTELLIGENCE

Originally started in recruitment and executive search, talent intelligence (TI) began by tracking top talent and benchmark salaries. Over time, it evolved into a data-driven discipline, providing skill-related insights, integrating internal workforce data with real-time labour market insights to guide hiring, retention and increasingly broader WFP and workforce strategy.[3] TI typically sits in Talent Acquisition, PA or Market Research teams. Unlike talent analytics, which focuses on internal workforce trends, TI adds an external perspective, analysing industry hiring patterns, competitor moves and hot skills demands to keep businesses ahead of competition.

ASSESSMENT

Assessment is all about understanding people's skills, strengths, personalities and how well they fit into the organization.[4] Through assessment, HR teams can get a clear picture of employees or job candidates through tools like skills tests, personality surveys, interviews and performance checks. It helps organizations figure out who might succeed, who needs extra support and where talent gaps might exist.

Assessment goes hand-in-hand with PA, with PA often leveraging assessment data to generate team, function or organization-wide insights.

ORGANIZATIONAL NETWORK ANALYSIS

Organizational Network Analysis (ONA) is an emerging field of research that often sits in PA. It studies how employees interact, collaborate and share information within an organization by analysing communication patterns, workflows and networks.[5]

While traditional HR analytics focuses on reporting structures, ONA uncovers hidden influencers, bottlenecks and collaboration trends,[6] offering insights into productivity, leadership effectiveness and team dynamics. Often applied within PA, IT, Communications and Real Estate teams, ONA helps organizations optimize workforce structures, improve cross-functional collaboration and enhance decision-making by revealing how information flows and where and how work gets done.

EMPLOYEE EXPERIENCE ANALYTICS

Employee experience analytics (EX), sometimes called employee engagement or employee listening, focuses on understanding the experience of being an employee throughout the employment lifecycle. It draws on both passive and active listening methods to explore employees' interactions with their workplace, culture, and tools.[7] It is often a subfunction of PA but can also exist as a standalone function or sit within other HR teams, such as Employee Experience, HR Operations or Talent Management.

The employee engagement/experience survey is a key instrument and data source in this field, taking various forms such as annual engagement surveys, frequent pulse checks, entry and exit surveys, and candidate experience surveys. While PA tracks retention and workforce trends, EX analytics delves deeper – leveraging both active listening (e.g. surveys and feedback tools) and passive listening (e.g. behavioural and sentiment data) – to help organizations enhance engagement, wellbeing and performance.

REWARD AND REMUNERATION ANALYTICS

Reward and remuneration analytics focuses on designing fair, competitive and performance-driven compensation structures using data.[8] It typically sits within Total Rewards teams and involves activities such as pay benchmarking, pay equity analysis, incentive design, salary forecasting and compensation modelling.

Unlike PA, which looks at workforce trends broadly, reward analytics is highly specialized, dealing specifically with pay structures and benefits design. While PA may explore how compensation impacts retention or performance, reward analytics focuses on internal salary positioning, external market competitiveness and predictive modelling for future compensation strategies.

> **TOP TIP**
> Clarify the context
>
> Definitions of these terms can vary between organizations, so do not assume your organization will use them in the way they are described here. In meetings, use clarifying questions like:
>
> • 'Am I correct in understanding that what you mean by "Talent analytics" covers the full spectrum of HR functions?'
> • 'Help me understand the "HR analytics" you referred to in this scenario…'

How are PA functions organized?

There's no right way to structure a PA function – the functional structures vary based on industry, company size and business alignment, according to different business priorities and workforce challenges. Here, we'll consider how they can differ according to company size, functional alignment and industry.

Company size

PA structures evolve as companies grow, shifting from generalist roles to specialized functions.

Small businesses typically rely on HR generalists using simple dashboards for Core HR metrics, turnover and compliance tracking.

Mid-sized companies introduce HR analysts who balance operational reporting with analytics, focusing on data visualization and trend forecasting. These companies are more likely to have 'full stack' PA professionals who have practitioner experience in all areas of the analytics lifecycle.

Larger companies often develop specialized PA teams, structured in different ways:

- Geo-based teams for regional workforce insights.
- Function-aligned teams (Centres of Excellence) specializing in areas like recruitment, engagement and DEI.
- Capability-aligned teams dividing PA teams into business partnering, modelling and analysis, and data infrastructure.
- Matrix structures that blend the above to respond to projects and requests while balancing strategic alignment and scalability.

A common misconception is that as companies grow, their PA naturally progresses from basic reporting to predictive insights. Smaller companies can often execute advanced analytics projects more efficiently because they have cleaner data, greater agility, and fewer bureaucratic barriers. Meanwhile, larger organizations frequently get stuck in HR reporting, struggling with fragmented systems, data silos and complex structures. Even with dedicated analytics teams, many big companies spend more time cleaning and integrating data than generating real strategic insights.[9]

Functional alignment

PA teams can sit in HR, IT, data functions or business units, each with its trade-offs. HR-aligned teams stay close to workforce challenges but often struggle with advanced analytics due to limited data literacy. IT or data-aligned teams have strong technical capabilities but risk becoming disconnected from real people problems, focusing more on systems, compliance and governance than practical insights. Business-embedded teams align directly with operational goals but can lack a broader strategic view. Many companies adopt a hybrid model, balancing technical expertise with business relevance to drive meaningful workforce insights.[10]

Industry

Industry priorities directly influence how PA teams are structured and resourced. In technology and financial services, where competition for top talent is high, PA teams often focus on talent acquisition, retention strategies and workforce productivity. These industries typically invest in dedicated PA teams with advanced capabilities, including predictive modelling and AI-driven insights.

In retail and hospitality, where large hourly workforces and high turnover are common, PA functions are often embedded within HR operations or workforce planning functions, prioritizing staffing optimization, attrition analysis, absenteeism and labour forecasting to meet business demand.

For healthcare and manufacturing, compliance, safety and operational efficiency take precedence. PA teams in these sectors are frequently aligned with HR, compliance or operational risk functions, focusing on workforce scheduling, regulatory adherence and training effectiveness.

Ultimately, industry context shapes the focus, structure and capabilities of PA teams, determining whether they operate as standalone functions, integrate into HR or operations, or collaborate across multiple business areas.

TOP TIP
Understand the organization chart

Before stepping into a PA role, figure out where the role may fit. Are you the first PA hire, expected to build processes from scratch, or part of a larger team with specialized roles? Do you sit within

HR, or are you embedded in a business function? Understanding your position in the organization chart helps you align expectations, focus your work, and navigate stakeholders effectively.

A brief history of PA and its evolution

'Look to the past to guide the future.' – Confucius

For early-career professionals, understanding the history of PA helps separate timeless principles from outdated practices so you can understand where ideas have come from and which still hold value. The field has evolved over a century, shaped by scientific management, workforce psychology and technology.

PA's origins can be traced back to 1911 with Frederick Taylor's *The Principles of Scientific Management*, which introduced systematic work measurement.[11] By the mid-20th century, industrial-organizational psychology focused on analysing employee behaviour, but HR remained administrative, focused on payroll and compliance.

The late 20th century saw the rise of HR information systems (HRIS)[12] and workforce analytics platforms, shifting HR from record-keeping to data-driven decision-making.

By understanding this evolution, you can diagnose your organization's PA maturity and understand what you may benefit from learning from your peers. Now, let us deep dive into the history of PA to see how it has shaped today's practices and where it is heading next.

Technology and PA (systems lens)

Technology has been a key driver in the evolution of PA, shaping what data can be captured, analysed and applied to workforce decisions. Each era of HR systems has expanded analytics capabilities, from basic record-keeping to AI-driven insights.

- **Pre-2000s – the age of manual entry and paper trails:** HR relied on paper files and spreadsheets,[13] and the more advanced companies tracked basic metrics like headcount and turnover. Data collection was infrequent and decisions were driven by intuition rather than analytics. Without modern databases, reporting was manual and time-consuming, and HR's role was mostly administrative.

- **Early 2000s – the rise of HRIS:** The introduction of enterprise HR systems (for example, PeopleSoft and Oracle) centralized records and digitized HR data. Applicant tracking systems (ATS) became common in recruitment. However, analytics remained descriptive and HR data was still siloed, with many companies operating in offline spreadsheets. HR information was not fully digitized, limiting insights.

- **2010s–2020 – unified HR platforms concept gains popularity:** There was a major push to consolidate HR systems under platforms like Workday and SuccessFactors to create a single source of truth.[14] However, due to the significant cost, not many organizations followed through with the transformation before the challenge posed by the rise of Application Programming Interfaces (APIs) (refer to Chapter 7 for more on APIs) and data connectors, which enabled organizations to integrate multiple best-in-class tools nimbly without sacrificing functionality. At the same time, HR was pushed to become 'data-driven' rather than reliant on intuition. The rise of descriptive analysis and dashboarding positioned data as the ultimate decision-making tool. However, the subsequent development revealed that data and intuition are not mutually exclusive, and the best organizations blended both to become truly data-informed – a theme explored further in later chapters.

- **2020–2021 – Covid-19 and the acceleration of digital adoption:** The pandemic forced rapid HR digital transformation, making HRIS, modern workplace tools and cloud-based analytics tools essential.[15] Real-time or close-to-real-time workforce data became critical for managing remote work, tracking wellbeing and adapting to disruptions. Previously slow adopters of digital HR tools felt forced to fully embrace HRIS and the benefits of PA. Data from digital collaboration tools such as Slack and Microsoft Teams became more mainstream, helping leaders monitor engagement and productivity in a virtual working world.

- **2022–2024 – Post-Covid-19 shifts and skills gain traction:** As economies slowed and the priorities shifted from recruitment and DEI to cost optimization and workforce efficiency, PA teams shrank in some organizations. At the same time, skills took centre stage with the heightened importance of workforce planning, with companies focusing on identifying skills gaps, reskilling employees and internal talent mobility. PA was now crucial in mapping capabilities and predicting future skill needs.

- **2025 onwards – AI, ethics and safeguarding the humanness in us:** The next phase can be driven by AI, automation and ethics. AI-powered tools have the potential to complete tasks at speed and scale, including but not limited to predicting flight risks, recommending career paths, and evaluating the systematic impact of people-related decisions in real time, with the potential of changing the PA role completely.

PA teams (people lens)

Initially, PA did not exist as a dedicated function; HR generalists handled workforce data as a side task. As organizations started to recognize PA's value, they began investing in specialized individuals, which evolved into teams that have grown in size and sophistication.

- **From lone wolves to growing teams:** A study by Insight222 of 184 companies found that the median PA team grew from one analyst per 4,000 employees in 2020 to 1 per 2,900 in 2021, a significant expansion. For a company with 100,000 employees, this meant a growth from 25 to 34 analysts in one year.[16]

- **Specialization and varied capabilities:** Early PA teams were made up of HR reporting specialists. Today, mature teams include data scientists, consultants, behavioural scientists, data engineers and visualization experts, allowing for more advanced workforce insights.[17]
- **Shifting team structures:** While PA teams originally sat within HR, many now report to a Chief Data Officer with a dotted line or are embedded in business units to align insights with broader company goals.[18] The trend features centralized Centres of Excellence, partnering with HR leaders and business executives to integrate workforce intelligence into strategy.

PA work (process and tasks lens)

There is a lot of talk about advanced analytics in PA – machine learning, predictive models, AI-driven workforce planning – but the reality inside most organizations is far less glamorous. Despite the excitement around innovative techniques, most PA work is still focused on operational reporting and non-predictive analysis.

This has less to do with technology limitations and more to do with HR's overall maturity in consuming and delivering insights. While businesses might invest in sophisticated HR platforms, many HR teams are still building the foundational skills needed to interpret and act on advanced analytics. As a result, PA teams often find themselves spending more time on standard HR reporting than on predictive modelling.

A reason for this misconception is survivorship bias; case studies and industry discussions highlight tech-forward projects, while routine tasks like turnover reports, headcount tracking and compliance metrics rarely get attention. As a result, early-career professionals may overestimate the maturity of PA and assume AI-driven insights dominate the field when data wrangling, reporting and stakeholder communication remain the core responsibilities.

As an early career professional, it's crucial to understand these less glamorous aspects and set realistic expectations. Strong foundational skills in data management, reporting and stakeholder engagement are essential before moving into advanced analytics. From a practitioner's perspective, the 80/20 rule can be applied to PA work as follows:

- 80 per cent of PA work involves operational reporting, dashboards, and historical analysis – critical for fulfilling the everyday needs of customers.
- 20 per cent includes advanced analytics like predictive modelling and AI, which, while growing, are still not the primary focus.

So, how has PA work evolved?

- **Basic reporting:** The methods have changed from manual spreadsheets (pre-2000s) to structured HRIS reports (2000s) to real-time dashboards (2010s–present), but the core task of tracking headcount, hires, leavers and other compliance metrics remains.
- **Advanced analytics growth:** Predictive modelling gained traction in attrition forecasting and workforce planning (2010s) but remains limited by HR's ability to act on insights.[19] AI-driven analytics in skills mapping and talent strategy (post-2020s) is emerging but not yet scaled.

TOP TIP
The importance of operational reporting

Mastering operational reporting is just as important as learning advanced analytics. While advanced analytics using AI may boom in the future, data accuracy, usability and clear communication will remain essential for making insights actionable.

We may find that PA will shift beyond optimizing workforce decisions to safeguarding the 'humanness' of work. As AI and automation evolve the speed and scale of decision-making, PA must ensure that data-driven insights remain ethical, inclusive and people-centric. Rather than simply driving efficiency, PA will likely guard and ensure that technology enhances, rather than diminishes, wellbeing, fairness and meaningful career development.

EXERCISE

Consider your own PA function or a PA function you know of from a systems, people and work lens:

- How has it evolved? Has it followed the trajectory above or taken a different path?
- Does the 80/20 rule resonate with you? Do you, or the function as a whole, spend 80 per cent of your time on operational matters and 20 per cent of your time on advanced analytics?
- Are you aware of future growth plans for your PA function?

PA's scope beyond data and numbers

Understanding scope is key to understanding what PA (or any other field) truly is.

PA sits at the intersection between people, data and business strategy. Without clear scope, analytics can become detached from real business needs, producing insights that leaders cannot act on.

This section lays the foundation for understanding PA, how defining scope, applying human-centred design and clarifying services ensure analytics delivers meaningful impact, not just data for data's sake. In this section, I want to highlight the importance of realistic scoping, balancing technical and human skills and setting expectations. This is because human insight is just as crucial as data expertise.

Why does scope management matter?

Defining the scope of PA work is critical to success. Without it, analytics teams risk either trying to do everything and failing or focusing on low-value issues. Effective scope management means choosing the right questions that need answering and the right problems to solve, because resources are limited and not every analysis will drive impact.

A common issue is a lack of focus. HR analytics teams can get overwhelmed with a series of interconnected problems, trying to solve attrition, hiring, engagement and every other workforce issue at once, leading to scattered efforts and no clear wins.

Another challenge is that PA professionals often deal with 'the middleman' – HR business partners or functional leaders – rather than the actual end users of their insights. This makes it difficult to balance between 'telling' leaders what the data reveals and asking what they truly need. Without direct access to decision-makers, analytics teams may focus on what stakeholders think they need, rather than uncovering the challenges of the end customers' needs.

Scope management keeps PA strategic, actionable and focused on business priorities – ensuring that insights drive real change rather than getting lost in reporting for reporting's sake. In this section, we will highlight strategies to clarify scope to help you set the foundation right from the beginning, personally and professionally.

TOP TIP
Understand scope for personal success

For you as an early-career professional, understanding scope is key to:

- Personal career growth – if you want to develop data science and advanced analytics skills but end up in a reporting-heavy role, the misalignment can slow your learning.

- Professional success – a well-defined scope helps set realistic expectations for your team's impact, ensuring efforts focus on high-value insights that leaders can act on.

Introduction to human-centred design principles

Human-centred design (HCD): A way of designing products and services that focuses on the end-user, prioritizing their needs, motivations and behaviours.[20]

HCD ensures solutions are useful, intuitive and actionable by focusing on user needs rather than just technical capability. It shifts PA from 'what we can build' to 'what people will actually use'. It can result in significantly higher adoption and better usability. As a concept, HCD underpins the entirety of this book. By embedding HCD principles, PA teams can shift from an isolated data team to a business-aligned function and achieve tangible impact and real value.

HCD is a powerful tool for scoping PA work, whether defining a team's function or an individual role. It ensures solutions are aligned with business needs, helping analytics teams focus on actionable insights rather than just producing technically sound models that no one uses.

For individual PA roles, HCD can teach you iteration and adaptability. Roles should evolve based on feedback and business needs, ensuring they deliver impact. Engaging with key stakeholders helps align responsibilities with challenges, rather than being constrained by a rigid job description.

Setting a PA function's scope requires two steps:

1 Understand user needs by engaging with key stakeholders, whether HR, business leaders or managers (stakeholder identification is covered in Chapter 3). Instead of assuming

what analytics should deliver, scope the function based on how insights will be used in practice.

2 Co-design the functional priorities with stakeholders. Instead of structuring a team solely on technical expertise, involve key users in decisions such as defining priorities, mapping workflows and testing small-scale analytics projects before scaling up.

DETERMINE YOUR SERVICE CATALOGUE

A service catalogue helps define and brand analytics offerings and prevent scope creep. It ensures that analytics efforts align with business priorities rather than becoming an operational reporting service.

A strong service catalogue organizes PA offerings into clear, structured services, helping the team proactively manage requests and communicate value. Deloitte's research on high-impact PA highlights how leading teams tailor their services to different audiences.[21] For example:

· Quarterly workforce planning insights for executives.
· Self-service dashboards with consulting support for HRBPs.
· One-off research for the Recruitment Director.

This segmentation ensures PA will be viewed as a strategic enabler rather than a reactive data provider.

So, how do we create a service catalogue? It can start at both the functional and individual levels:

· Functional perspective: If you are setting up the PA function, start with grouping the current service requirements based on similarity, then assign each service group a value score determined on demand and impact. Then use the 'stop-start-continue' framework with the stakeholders to co-create the service catalogue by matching service group and internal resource and requests for additional resources if budget allows. Establish clear service tiers with different service level agreements (SLA) such as self-service tools, advisory support and strategic insights, ensuring alignment with key business priorities (more in Chapter 8).

- Individual perspective: Even if you are not defining the entire function's offerings, structuring your own scope is critical. For example, if you specialize in recruitment analytics, you can group your services as 'Operational Self-Service Reports', 'Ad hoc Insights Requests' and 'Advanced Analytics Offerings'. This clarifies expectations and prevents ad-hoc, low-impact work from consuming valuable time.

A well-communicated service catalogue also acts as an internal marketing tool, making it clear how PA contributes to business success. Leading teams continuously reiterate and adapt their catalogue to stay relevant, ensuring their analytics remain actionable and aligned with evolving stakeholder needs (more on branding in Chapter 2).

Balancing people and technical skills

As mentioned in the Introduction, one of the biggest misconceptions about entering the field of PA is that analytical skills outweigh people skills. Many assume practitioners must be data gurus, when success actually comes from building trust through understanding business needs, engaging stakeholders and communicating insights effectively.

The surge in technical training in things like Python, R and machine learning has led some to place more importance on tools than impact. Job advertisements list advanced machine learning and predictive analytics as required skills, even though these are rarely used in practice. Too often, newcomers (and even organizations) become so fixated on technical capabilities that they overlook the bigger picture. Many experience a reality check when they realize that no matter how advanced an analysis is, if it does not address a real need or is not used by decision-makers, it has little value.

This challenge is amplified in HR, where data literacy tends to be lower than in other business functions. Many HR stakeholders need more support, clearer explanations and practical takeaways to engage with analytics effectively. The reality check moment happens when a team presents a sophisticated model that took months to perfect, only to hear, 'I don't understand, and you don't seem to be able to explain your own model to me. How can I act on this?' Without business context, stakeholder buy-in and clear communication, even the most advanced analytics cannot prove itself.

Western business thinking, particularly in the United States and Europe, prioritizes data-driven decisions, while Eastern philosophies, such as those in China and Japan, value trust and influence.[22] Straddling the line between logic and emotion, PA must bridge both to ensure insights are not only credible but also understandable and drive action. Focusing only on technical mastery can risk producing impressive but unused analyses. Relying only on relationships, especially in fast-changing Western workplaces, can be exhausting without data-backed credibility. The most successful PA professionals balance both, ensuring their insights are trusted, understood and acted upon.

TOP TIP
Which tools should I learn?

It might be tempting to jump into Python, R or machine learning because they sound impressive. Before you go there, get very, very good at Excel first.

Excel is not just a basic spreadsheet tool; it is a powerful analytics engine when used effectively. Mastering pivot tables, pivot charts, Power Query, complex nested formulas and financial modelling will give you the core analytical foundation that applies across any tool. Many advanced analytics techniques can be replicated in Excel, and a strong grasp of these concepts will make learning other tools easier.

Think you are already good at Excel? Think again. The Dunning-Kruger effect, where beginners overestimate their abilities, may apply. Many people believe they know Excel because they can use SUMIF or VLOOKUP. But true mastery means:

- Building dynamic dashboards using pivot tables and slicers.

- Automating data cleaning with Power Query.

- Writing deeply nested formulas that replace manual work.

- Understanding financial modelling techniques that improve workforce planning.

Once you have a solid Excel foundation, progress to SQL, Python or R. But don't overlook Excel. It remains one of the most used tools in PA, given its speed, flexibility and understandability by HR teams.

Test yourself:

- Could you build an interactive workforce report entirely in Excel?

- Could you clean and merge datasets without opening another tool?

If not, your learning journey should start here.

Seven habits of highly effective PA professionals

The list below is inspired by Stephen Covey's book, *The Seven Habits of Highly Effective People*. By adopting these, you can move beyond producing reports to truly driving impact and influencing decisions.

HABIT 1: ENGAGE STAKEHOLDERS EARLY

- Do: Involve HR, business leaders and managers from the start to ensure insights address real needs.

- Don't: Work in isolation, producing reports that no one asked for or understands.

HABIT 2: FOCUS ON OUTCOMES, NOT JUST OUTPUTS

- Do: Measure success by business impact (e.g. reduced turn-over, better hiring, improved engagement).
- Don't: Focus only on the volume of delivered dashboards, models or reports, without ensuring they lead to action.

HABIT 3: TRANSLATE DATA INTO STORIES

- Do: Simplify insights and tell compelling stories that non-technical leaders can understand and act on.
- Don't: Overwhelm stakeholders with complex models, statistics and technical jargon.

HABIT 4: BUILD TRUST THROUGH SMALL WINS

- Do: Establish credibility by delivering quick, visible wins before proceeding with complex projects.
- Don't: Expect instant recognition based on technical expertise alone.

HABIT 5: MAKE INSIGHTS PRACTICAL AND ACTIONABLE

- Do: Provide clear, concrete recommendations and next steps tailored to the audience.
- Don't: Leave decision-makers unsure of what to do with the data.

HABIT 6: DEVELOP BOTH TECHNICAL AND BUSINESS ACUMEN

- Do: Balance data skills with HR knowledge and strategic thinking to ensure insights align with business needs.
- Don't: Either over-focus on technical skills without business understanding, or lack data literacy altogether.

HABIT 7: UPSTREAM/DOWNSTREAM FORESIGHT

- Do: Integrate insights into existing HR and business processes so they naturally inform decisions.
- Don't: Create standalone reports that require extra effort to access and use, leading to low adoption.

EXERCISE

How effective is your PA team (or the one you are preparing to work with)? Use the list as a diagnostic tool to understand where improvements could be made.

Avoid the single point of failure trap

Single point of failure: A part of a system, such as a person or process, that, if it stops working, causes the whole system to break down, making the success of the system dependent on that one part.[23]

Becoming a single point of failure is a major risk in PA. Too often, expertise can become concentrated in one person or a small group. If that person or people leave, get overloaded or priorities shift, progress stalls.

For individuals, this can mean long-term career stagnation, getting stuck in operational tasks instead of strategic work. It can also mean being constantly pulled into work, even on holidays.

For teams, failing to share knowledge and integrate with HR and business functions makes PA vulnerable to budget cuts, limited influence or being sidelined. If only one or two experts handle models, reporting or insights, the team becomes a bottleneck rather than a value driver.

To avoid the single point of failure trap, you can try the following strategies:

- Cross-skill within your team: Ensure multiple people can handle key responsibilities, reducing dependency on any one individual.
- Document and share knowledge: Maintain clear records of key processes, models and reports so work can continue smoothly if someone steps away.
- Rotate projects among team members: As a leader, encourage learning by involving different people in various tasks to prevent single-person reliance.
- Automate and scale wisely: Build self-service dashboards and automated reports so HR and business teams can access operational metrics independently.
- Avoid taking full ownership of projects not initiated by PA: If a request comes from another function, set clear boundaries on your role as a supporter rather than the owner. Define what is and is not within scope to prevent PA from being pulled into ongoing maintenance work beyond their role.
- Build HR data literacy: Regularly train HR business partners on basic analytics so they can interpret and use data without always relying on the PA team.

The strongest PA professionals and teams balance deep expertise with adaptability, ensuring they are resilient, indispensable and able to fully disconnect from work when needed.

CHAPTER SUMMARY

- PA can mean different things to different people and organizations, and it is related to many fields such as workforce planning and talent intelligence. Fundamentally, it's a systematic approach to using people data to generate value.
- PA functions can be structured in different ways depending on company size, industry and alignment with other functions.
- PA has evolved over a century. Its history can be viewed through people, systems and process lenses.

- Managing the scope of your PA function is critical to its ability to deliver value. Human-centred design is a useful tool for defining a team's function or an individual's role.

- Success in PA requires more than technical skills, it demands business understanding, communication and influence. Many early-career professionals focus on coding and dashboards, but without the ability to translate insights into action, technical skills have limited impact.

REVIEW QUESTIONS

1 What's the difference between PA, HR analytics and WFP?

2 Why is a balanced approach important for PA (balancing technical and people skills)?

3 What are some effective methods to manage the scope of your work?

Endnotes

1 Król, K and Zdonek, D (2020) Analytics Maturity Models: An Overview, *Information*, 11(3), 142, www.mdpi.com/2078-2489/11/3/142 (archived at https://perma.cc/7E9M-LYR3)

2 Human Capital Institute (2015) Strategic Workforce Planning Participant Guide, p 22

3 Beamery (2024) Talent Intelligence Explained: Unlocking The Power of Data In HR, Beamery, https://beamery.com/resources/talent-operations/what-is-talent-intelligence (archived at https://perma.cc/68UZ-Z9L7)

4 AIHR (2025) Employee Skills Assessment: How to Measure Competencies, AIHR, https://www.aihr.com/blog/employee-skills-assessment/ (archived at https://perma.cc/D45Q-U2A3)

5 Zielinski, D (2018) Find Your Influencers with Organizational Network Analysis, SHRM, https://www.shrm.org/topics-tools/news/technology/find-influencers-organizational-network-analysis (archived at https://perma.cc/BY7H-L237)

6 Zielinski, D (2018) Find Your Influencers with Organizational Network Analysis, SHRM, https://www.shrm.org/topics-tools/news/technology/find-influencers-organizational-network-analysis (archived at https://perma.cc/BY7H-L237)

7 Perceptyx (2022) From Measurement to Problem Solving: The Role of Continuous Listening, Perceptyx, https://blog.perceptyx.com/from-measurement-to-problem-solving-the-role-of-continuous-listening (archived at https://perma.cc/RPG9-RPZM)

8 Compensation and Benefits: The Complete Guide, AIHR, https://www.aihr.com/blog/compensation-and-benefits/ (archived at https://perma.cc/2Z2G-JQGE)

9 LinkedIn (2023) What Are the Common Pitfalls and Barriers to Implementing and Scaling HR Analytics Initiatives?, LinkedIn, https://www.linkedin.com/advice/1/what-common-pitfalls-barriers-implementing-scaling (archived at https://perma.cc/WR5V-TAJR)

10 AIHR (2023) 4 People Analytics Operating Models to Implement, AIHR, https://www.aihr.com/blog/people-analytics-operating-models/ (archived at https://perma.cc/8HPJ-ALCD)

11 Taylor, F W (1911) *The Principles of Scientific Management*, Harper & Brothers

12 Bhuiyan, F, Chowdhury, M M and Ferdous, F (2014) Historical Evolution of Human Resource Information System (HRIS): An Interface between HR and Computer Technology, *Human Resource Management Research*, 4(4), 75–80, https://article.sapub.org/10.5923.j.hrmr.20140404.01.html (archived at https://perma.cc/YST7-6AP2)

13 Ubisend (2019) The History of Technology in Human Resources, Ubisend Blog, https://blog.ubisend.com/discover-chatbots/history-of-technology-in-human-resources (archived at https://perma.cc/P3CP-5LSA)

14 Bersin, J (2010) The Evolution of HR Systems: Update from HR Technology Conference 2010, Josh Bersin, https://joshbersin.com/2010/10/the-evolution-of-hr-systems-update-from-hr-technology-conference-2010/ (archived at https://perma.cc/9JEF-TF47)

15 Conference Board (2020) Covid-19 Reset and Recovery: A Look into Digital HR Technology and Operations, The Conference Board, https://www.conference-board.org/publications/digital-HR-Tech-and-Ops (archived at https://perma.cc/Q4XC-LU7H)

16 Ferrar, J, González Sedano, N and Verghese, N (2022) People Analytics Trends 2022: Impacting Business Value, Insight222, publications.insight222.com/peopleanalyticstrends2022 (archived at https://perma.cc/KJF7-S8HE)

17 Insights222 (2024) The Core Roles of a High-Performing People Analytics Team, myHRfuture, https://www.myhrfuture.com/blog/the-core-roles-of-a-high-performing-people-analytics-team (archived at https://perma.cc/EL2Z-ETDH)

18 Patel, K (2023) How to Build a Modern Data Team: Structure, Skill Sets and Common Mistakes, ThoughtSpot, https://www.thoughtspot.com/data-trends/how-to-build-a-modern-data-team-structure-skill-sets-and-common-mistakes (archived at https://perma.cc/B6XD-KFQW)

19 Nalla, N (2024) Predictive HR Analytics: Forecasting Workforce Needs with AI and Big Data, ResearchGate, https://www.researchgate.net/publication/390480537_Predictive_HR_Analytics (archived at https://perma.cc/9MSB-KS2V)

20 Interaction Design Foundation (nd) What Is Human-Centered Design (HCD)?, Interaction Design Foundation, https://www.interaction-design.org/literature/topics/human-centered-design (archived at https://perma.cc/5RVY-FF3B)

21 Deloitte (2023) High-Impact People Analytics, Deloitte, 14 November, www2.deloitte.com/us/en/pages/human-capital/articles/high-impact-people-analytics.html (archived at https://perma.cc/3HUA-3XUW)

22 Mandarin Blueprint (2023) 9 Key Differences Between Western and Chinese Business Culture, Mandarin Blueprint, https://www.mandarinblueprint.com/blog/9-key-differences-between-western-and-chinese-business-culture/ (archived at https://perma.cc/EMU3-C47R)

23 Kirvan, P and Bigelow, S J (2020) What Is A Single Point of Failure (SPOF) and How to Avoid Them?, TechTarget, www.techtarget.com/searchdatacenter/definition/Single-point-of-failure-SPOF (archived at https://perma.cc/7VJA-9LUC)

CHAPTER TWO

People analytics branding via systems thinking

Introduction

Two secret weapons will set high-performing PA professionals apart: systems thinking and branding. Systems thinking helps us to solve problems by understanding how the different parts of an organization interact, influence each other and produce both intended and unintended outcomes. Branding is the act of making something (or someone) easily recognizable by connecting it with certain attributes or features.

For early-career professionals, focusing on these two foundational elements is critical for your career growth and ensuring your work drives real impact. Without a strong grasp of how business functions are interconnected, analytics efforts risk becoming isolated exercises rather than strategic enablers. And without a strong understanding of branding and the importance of customers, PA efforts risk becoming self-reinforcing fallacies.

An ancient Chinese concept called 'strategic force' emphasizes applying force wisely, with precision in strength and timing to achieve more with less. It's useful to view this alongside the 80/20 principle, which reminds us that success often comes from focusing on the 20 per cent of effort that drives 80 per cent of the outcome. For PA, branding and systems thinking belong in that 20 per cent. That is why they appear early in the book, because setting the right direction is often more valuable than sprinting in every direction.

This chapter begins with branding. We consider its importance for PA and look at how to build a successful PA brand, distinguishing between internal, external and personal brands. We then move on to systems thinking, a concept which underpins much of the rest of this book. We then bring branding and systems thinking together to create a 90-day roadmap for building a strong PA brand.

> **Branding:** making something (or someone) easily recognizable by connecting it with different attributes or features.[1]

> **Systems thinking:** a way of thinking that considers how different elements interact, influence each other and produce intended and unintended outcomes.[2]

LEARNING OBJECTIVES

By the end of this chapter, you will be able to:

- Explain the importance of branding for PA and how to strengthen your internal, external and personal brand.
- Articulate how systems thinking can be applied to PA and give examples to demonstrate its value.
- Explain the relationship between systems thinking and building a strong brand.
- Put together a 90-day roadmap to strengthen your PA brand.

Branding for PA

Branding is important for any business and individuals. Strong brands are trusted by their customers and build non-transactional relationships. They are easily recognizable and don't have to explain what they do. Instead of pushing services to customers, customers seek out strong brands to satisfy their needs.[3] This is a self-reinforcing cycle, continuously strengthening the brand's value and its trust with its customers.

To understand the power of branding as a high-leverage capability, look no further than Apple. In an industry where many companies compete on technical specifications, price or promotional tactics, Apple has consistently stood apart by prioritizing brand. It represents 20 per cent of the effort that generates 80 per cent of the impact.[4]

Unlike competitors that push products onto customers through aggressive sales strategies, Apple pulls customers into a carefully curated ecosystem and lifestyle. Its branding is not just about marketing or aesthetics, it shapes product design, user experience, store layout, packaging and even customer service. The result is a seamless and emotionally resonant experience that makes customers feel part of something more than just a product.[5]

Apple demonstrates how a deep understanding of customers, combined with long-term brand strategy, can drive sustainable differentiation, not by doing more, but by doing the right things with clarity and consistency. These same qualities make high-performing PA teams stand out. These teams are known internally as trusted strategic partners and externally as best-in-class examples of the discipline. The practitioners behind them are frequently consulted on how to build and scale effective PA functions. Internally, the teams attract problem-solving opportunities rather than reporting requests. Like Apple, these teams don't need to chase visibility, they earn it by consistently delivering meaningful value at the right place and the right time.

Why is PA branding important?

PA branding is about shaping the perception of you and your function in the eyes of your internal and external stakeholders, customers and partners. Branding is not only shaped by logos, colours or presentation slides, but also by reputation, influence and trust.[6] Branding in PA shapes the kinds of opportunities you are given, how seriously your insights are taken and whether you are seen as a service function or a strategic partner. Like Apple, high-performing PA teams stand out because they have a clear identity and consistent delivery, which attracts meaningful problems to solve rather than reactive reporting tasks.

STOP AND THINK

In 12 months, what do you want your internal and external stakeholders to think and say about you and your function? What emotions or feelings should go through their minds when they think of your work? When your name is brought up in a room that you are not in, what will they say about you?

WHY WON'T THE WORK SPEAK FOR ITSELF?

Good work is not automatically recognized. Early in your career, this can be difficult to get your head around. It's easy to believe that if someone's work is consistently high quality, people will eventually notice.

Work rarely speaks for itself unless it has the right surrounding environment.[7] In large organizations where attention is scarce and priorities shift quickly, excellent work often ends up in the 'not so useful' basket, simply because it wasn't seen, understood or championed at the right level. In environments like these, influence drives decisions as much as, sometimes more than, evidence of hard work. A talented analyst could build a complex, high-value model that could save their business hundreds of thousands of pounds. But if they don't have direct access to decision-makers, their insights may never make it past their own laptop. Their work and their brilliance will get lost in layers of middle management between them and those who could act, diluted by politics, egos and organizational hierarchies.

This is why branding matters. Not for show, but to make sure that the value you create reaches the people who need to see it. You can build the most insightful slide deck or the slickest dashboards, but if you have no audience, the effort you put into building these fantastic user-ready products will do nothing more than help you practice the skills you already have.

This doesn't mean self-promotion for the sake of ego. It means making sure your work is understood, contextualized and connected to the people it is meant to help. Studies from Harvard Business School[8] and CIPD[9] have consistently shown that the most effective PA functions invest heavily in stakeholder engagement, internal storytelling and reputation-building alongside technical excellence.

Understanding branding gives you a huge advantage, helping to shift your mindset from just 'doing the work' to 'doing the right work'. You are not just delivering data. You are shaping decisions, relationships and organizational outcomes, all of which are influenced by the strength of your brand.

How to build a strong PA brand

Building a strong PA brand relies on understanding who has power and influence and asking for people's attention.

UNDERSTANDING WHERE POWER LIES

Understanding where the power lies will help you build your brand along the path of least resistance. Instead of pushing your work uphill in all directions, hoping it will be noticed, you can align yourself with the people and moments that unlock opportunity and momentum.

TOP TIP
Where does the power lie?

Pay attention to dynamics in the room. Who holds influence? Who has the final say? Who moves things forward, and who merely speaks the loudest? Building this awareness allows you to spend less time on non-productive tasks and more time getting things done with the right people involved from the start.

Power in organizations doesn't always follow the hierarchy. Titles matter, yes, but so do relationships, reputation and timing. Some people hold the purse strings. Others shape the story. Some have the authority to approve, while others have the soft power to influence. Mapping this landscape and understanding who matters to your work and, in turn, the individuals who matter to them, is one of the most overlooked but valuable habits in PA.

Below are five simple but powerful ways to start mapping influence and building your brand where it matters most:

1 **Follow the money**
   Pay attention to who controls the budget or can approve spending. These people often have decision-making power or influence over which projects move forward.

2 **Observe who gets mentioned when they're not in the room**
   If a name keeps coming up in meetings, emails or casual conversations, chances are that person holds influence formally or informally. If someone has no real power, people generally won't spend their time discussing them. Whether the mentions are positive or negative, it's a clear signal that this person is part of the decision-making group. It's a good idea to build direct rapport and understand their perspective.

3 **Watch who helps others**
   When problems come up or decisions stall, who do people turn to for advice or support? These are informal leaders, and

people owe them favours. A message delivered through them might have a multiplied effect.

4 **Identify key connectors**
Look for the people who seem to know everyone, are copied into everything or constantly make introductions. They are often trusted advisers or internal influencers. A conversation with them can help you quickly identify organizational dynamics and map out the easiest path to amplify the impact of your work.

5 **Listen and watch closely in meetings**
Who do people defer to? Who do they avoid contradicting? Watch the body language, tone and reactions. Influence often shows up more clearly in the dynamics than in job titles.

UNDERSTANDING ATTENTION

Attention is the mental availability people give to a specific person, idea or task. It is a finite resource that reflects what they perceive as relevant or important in a given moment.[10] In psychology and behavioural science, attention is often described as the gateway to perception, memory and action.[11] In practical terms, if you do not have someone's attention, your message, insight or even your presence does not register. It simply does not exist in their decision-making world.[12]

Many early-career professionals, especially those who are thoughtful and considerate, can assume senior leaders are too busy to engage with their work. They might not want to interrupt or 'bother' them.[13] This deprioritizes their own agenda before anyone else even sees it. The truth is, leader's calendars are often filled with surprisingly trivial matters such as recurring admin meetings, slide reviews and status catch-ups. Important things, yes, but not necessarily more important than the value you are trying to offer.

Your agenda and your brand matter. They only become unimportant when you decide they are. Sometimes, a little bit of blind confidence can be a powerful tool for someone who tends to overthink.[14] This is also where your passion comes in, your passion is the reason you chose PA in the first place. When you speak from that place, you become more compelling. People respond to energy and intent,[15] not just logic. Let your curiosity and belief in the work come through. That is how you make people care. You will find that if you let your natural energy flow, a brand that sticks will be built naturally.

TOP TIP
Prioritize your agenda

Be brave enough to take up space. Ask for a moment of attention. Not too much, just enough to show what you bring. And when you do, be sharp, clear and relevant.

Different types of brands for PA

PA branding can be categorized into three different types: internal, external and personal. Each plays a different role in shaping your reputation and career, and all three can be intentionally developed from the very beginning.

INTERNAL BRAND

Your internal brand is how people inside your organization perceive the PA function. It is the feelings that arise when 'PA' is said in a casual conversation.

How to strengthen it:

1 Build high-quality products that solve real problems: Prioritize projects that address stakeholder needs. Show how your work links to business outcomes, not just metrics.
2 Leverage internal influencers: Partner with individuals who are well-respected and well-connected. Their support helps your work travel further (more on this in Chapter 3).
3 Create a consistent look and feel: Use a clean, professional visual style for your reports and presentations that's

unique but aligns with your organization's templates. Work with the communications team/specialist to leverage their expertise.

4 Host internal thought leadership events: Get a slot in town halls, learning sessions or short talks to share your insights and educate others about what PA can do.

5 Run gamified learning experiences: Use competitions, quizzes or interactive tools to engage others in your work through making data approachable and exciting.

6 Build internal communities: Start informal networks for people interested in people data or behavioural science and create space for shared learning.

7 Offer training and upskilling: Empower others to understand and use data themselves. The more people are trained through these sessions, the stronger your brand becomes.

8 Send newsletters and internal thought leadership: Share short, engaging updates about your team's work and interesting findings. Highlight impact, progress and new projects in the pipeline.

9 Secure internal sponsorship: Build relationships with senior leaders who can champion your work and help position you as a trusted adviser.

EXTERNAL BRAND

Your external brand is how the broader professional community sees your organization's PA effort. It is about building a reputation outside your organization, among peers, potential collaborators and industry leaders. A strong external brand helps you stay current, grow your network and amplify your organization's brand.

How to strengthen it:

1 Participate in industry events: Attend or speak at HR/PA conferences and roundtables. These are great places to learn, share and connect.

2 Publish thought leadership: Share insights, reflections or case studies online. This helps you build a presence and contribute to the field.

3 Nominate for awards: Research industry awards and submit nominations on behalf of your organization. Many professionals self-nominate for awards. Simply applying can increase your exposure and credibility.

4 Secure external sponsorship: Build relationships with respected figures in the field who can endorse the organization's work publicly.

5 Contribute to professional communities: Join groups and forums focused on PA. Contribute actively by using PA cases from your organization.

PERSONAL BRAND

Your personal brand is the professional identity that belongs to you, not your team or organization. It reflects your values, strengths and point of view and travels with you throughout your career.[16] While internal and external brands often rely on the collective reputation of your team, your personal brand is entirely your own.

This distinction becomes especially important if you are a one-person PA team. In these cases, your work and identity can blur with the organization's, so building a personal brand helps create separation. It gives you a voice that exists outside your current role and helps you build long-term credibility in the field.

How to strengthen it:

1 Define what makes you different: Identify your niche, whether that's storytelling, data governance and ethics, analytics translation, technical excellence or a combination. Know what you bring to the table.

2 Be yourself: Your personal brand should be rooted in authenticity. Let your values and personality guide how

you show up, so your reputation is not only strong, but sustainable.

3   Be consistent across platforms: Make sure your LinkedIn, internal comms and conversations reflect your niche.

4   Stay active in external communities: Join networks, share insights and participate in conversations. This helps anchor your identity in the field, not just within your company.

5   Collaborate with external influencers: Partner with respected professionals on articles, webinars or community events to raise your visibility.

6   Offer pro bono support or mentoring: Whether it is helping an early-career professional or volunteering analytics support for a community cause, this builds a reputation for generosity and expertise.

7   Ask for feedback: Regular feedback helps you understand how you are perceived and where you can grow. Your personal brand is always evolving.

According to a Deloitte report, high-performing PA teams actively cultivate external networks for benchmarking and innovation.[17] So external brand and personal brand are not only a 'nice to have' in addition to internal brand.

TOP TIP
Just reach out

Start to build your network by following thought leaders in the PA field. Read their work and connect with like-minded people who are also following the thought leaders on LinkedIn. People are more open to connecting than you might expect. Most folks in the PA space are passionate about their work and happy to chat. The key is to be bold enough to make the first move. Don't wait until you're 'ready' or have something impressive to share. A well-crafted message showing interest in their work and your passion in the field can go a long way.

Systems thinking for PA

Systems thinking is the ability to understand how different parts of an organization interact, influence each other and produce both intended and unintended outcomes. Instead of looking at problems in isolation, systems thinking explores how processes, behaviours, feedback loops and environments are connected.[18]

Large organizations can sometimes be held back by internal politics, silos and short-term thinking.[19] Boeing, Microsoft (pre-Satya Nadella)[20] and GE during Jack Welsh's reign[21] are classic examples. While they all focused heavily on internal metrics and cost efficiency, neglecting the bigger picture led to strategic stagnation, reputational damage and, in Boeing's case, tragic safety failures.[22]

As PA professionals, we're uniquely positioned to spot these issues early and influence how the system operates. But to do that effectively, we need to move beyond basic reporting and start thinking in systems. This section introduces the basic concepts related to systems thinking. You will learn more about system-led ways of working through the subsequent chapters. Something important to note – in this chapter, we will cover only a few fundamental principles of systems thinking, just enough to provide you with a foundation and direction for further study. Systems thinking is a complex and nuanced field, and the content presented here is not intended to be comprehensive or fully representative of its depth.

Synthesis versus analysis

In many organizations, PA capabilities span across two functions. One focuses on analysis, which means breaking problems into components. The other leans into synthesis, which involves engaging the business, spotting patterns and helping stakeholders connect the dots.

While this approach plays to individual strengths, it often creates a disconnect. Insights get built, but are not always used.

It's the same issue software vendors face when sales and delivery are misaligned: you end up with outputs that don't match the real-world need.

Analysis is about isolating variables and examining them in detail. It helps answer specific questions. Synthesis, on the other hand, is about putting the puzzle back together. It looks at how the parts interact in a system.[23]

As an early-career professional, aim to build capability in both areas before specializing. Otherwise, you risk building for the sake of building, creating technically sound but strategically irrelevant work. Systems thinking requires both lenses. When analysis and synthesis come together,[24] PA becomes value-adding.

Feedback loops

In systems thinking, a feedback loop describes how an outcome in a system circles back to influence future behaviour. These loops can either reinforce a trend (making it stronger) or balance it out (bringing the system back into stability).[25]

Consider this example related to gender equity. Imagine a company where women are consistently placed in departments with lower promotion rates. Over time, these women begin to feel there's limited opportunity to grow. Some leave. As a result, there are even fewer women progressing into leadership roles. This reinforces the belief that there's a 'leaky pipeline' while women continue to be funnelled into those same low-opportunity areas. That's a reinforcing feedback loop in action. It starts as a structural imbalance, but becomes self-perpetuating. The system unknowingly reproduces inequality, not because anyone intends to, but because no one is tracking how the pieces influence one another.

In this case, PA can trigger a balancing feedback loop. By identifying the pattern and presenting the data, the team can make recommendations that influence changes in internal mobility practices, ensuring women are more equitably placed in high-opportunity areas. Leadership might introduce sponsorship schemes or targeted development programmes, which begin to shift promotion outcomes and retention. As more women progress and stay, the system starts to correct itself. This is systems thinking in action: recognizing how seemingly small imbalances can escalate and using data to introduce interventions that help the system stabilize and move towards equity.

> **Balancing feedback loop:** When an event happens within a system, it restores stability by counteracting any deviations from the desired state. It works against change by continuously offsetting the deviation to bring the system back to equilibrium. A balancing feedback loop often works to oppose the direction of change, guiding the system back to homeostasis.[26]

> **Homeostasis:** Another word you will hear in systems thinking that represents the stable state or equilibrium.[27]

> **Reinforcing feedback loop:** When an event within a system reinforces the original direction of momentum. Balancing feedback loop results in growth in a direction, each iteration of this event strengthens the current behaviour and it can lead to exponential growth or decline.[28]

Environments, boundaries and relationships

In systems thinking, environments, boundaries and relationships define the context in which behaviour and outcomes emerge.[29] No one operates in isolation. Every person's choices, performance and experience are shaped by the people around them, the systems they work in and the invisible structures that guide their day-to-day lives.

The journalist and author Malcolm Gladwell once wrote 'Don't look at the stranger and jump to conclusions. Look at the stranger's world'.[30] The same holds true in organizations. If someone is disengaged, struggling with performance or resisting change, it's rarely just about them. It's about the environment they operate in.

Boundaries refer to where we draw the line around what's included in our analysis.[31] If a PA team only looks at full-time employees, they might miss how contractors or external market dynamics are shaping workforce trends. If engagement is analysed by department, but cross-functional friction is never measured, we lose sight of what's really driving sentiment.

Relationships are the connective tissue. Who influences whom? Which teams collaborate well and which don't? Understanding how people, processes and teams are connected allows PA to move beyond static reporting and see how change moves through the system.

When PA professionals start mapping environments, questioning boundaries and studying relationships, they shift from producing isolated insights to offering system-level understanding. We cover more on how to do this in subsequent chapters.

Emergence

Mix blue and yellow and you don't get a more intense blue or a pale yellow, you get green. Something entirely new, something neither colour held on its own. That's a simple analogy to introduce you to the concept of emergence. It's when two or more elements interact and produce an unexpected outcome that can't be predicted by looking at the parts in isolation.[32]

Understanding the concept of emergence can help us keep our ego in check and let go the overrated concept of 'being right'. In PA, this matters more than we sometimes admit. It's incredibly easy to over-rely on 'what the data says', to treat insights as hard truths, to design confidently based on what worked last quarter or to present charts with absolute conviction. Human systems don't stand still. New conditions, new interactions and new behaviours emerge all the time.

Emergence teaches us humility. It reminds us that it is impossible to predict everything and it's best to stay adaptive and responsive.[33] Great PA work blends data with listening, curiosity and context. Because sometimes, what matters most isn't already on your dashboard, it's what's just starting to bubble up.

Putting branding and systems thinking together

A strong brand does not happen by accident. It's built through intentional moves that make a brand a part of someone's life experiences and critical moments. To understand this, we need to learn about systems thinking, because a brand is rarely built in isolation. It's built through understanding the environments its customers are in, the pain points associated with being in that environment and being remembered for relieving the pain at the right time.

This is where social engineering comes in in the broader behavioural systems sense. Social engineering is about shaping environments and interactions in a way that nudges people towards a certain perception or action.[34] In PA, branding yourself or your function isn't just about shouting on LinkedIn or putting out fancy dashboards. It's about engineering moments of value across touchpoints: how you present data, how you influence decision-makers, how others talk about you when you're not in the room. You're not just working within a system; you have the power to subtly shape it. As Donella Meadows, a leading authority on systems thinking described, the most powerful leverage points in a system often come from changing mindsets and narratives, not just processes.[35] A strong PA brand uses this thinking to embed itself in the flow of organizational life, influencing culture by being part of how decisions are made and understood.

Improving data literacy is a perfect example. When PA takes ownership of it using simple techniques such as running bite-sized learning sessions, building easy-to-follow guides, or just explaining the 'why' behind the numbers in everyday chats, it starts to shift how HR works. IT bakes data thinking into HR's day-to-day. That's systems thinking in action: one small, consistent change (like demystifying data) ends up shifting behaviours across the board.

And it doesn't stop there. It spreads. Other enabling functions will start picking up the same habits and mindset. Soon, the whole organization will be making smarter, data-informed decisions, often without realizing that PA helped get them there. But here's the thing, PA doesn't need all the credit. Because at that point, no one's debating whether the function is necessary or not. It just is. It's part of how the organization thinks, decides and moves forward.

STOP AND THINK

Consider your organization. Can you identify any opportunities to use your brand to change mindsets and narratives, as described in the data literacy example? Consider initiatives such as data governance, skills frameworks and workforce planning. How might you be able to help shift unhelpful behaviours?

Systems thinking can help you build something that lasts. When you think systemically, you stop chasing short-term wins and start creating long-term value.[36] You avoid falling into the traps that derail PA teams, such as low product adoption, reactive ad hoc work and burnout from trying to do everything for everyone.

More importantly, you build better relationships. Leaders start to trust you, not just because of the numbers you provide, but because of the insight and perspective you bring. They come to you not just for reports, but for direction. And that's when your personal brand starts to shift. You become known as someone who sees the bigger picture, who connects the dots and helps others make smarter, more sustainable decisions.

Integrating branding with systems thinking is how you make PA indispensable. Not through volume, speed or flashy dashboards, but by quietly reshaping how the organization understands itself.

So, if you're early in your PA journey, start with this mindset: you're not here just to fix. You're here to design. And systems thinking is your blueprint.

A roadmap to a strong PA brand

In a new PA role, your first 90 days are critical for shaping how you, your team and your work are perceived. Here is a simple 90-day roadmap example that will help you build trust, credibility and visibility in ways that are sustainable and valuable.

Weeks 1 to 4: Establish credibility and learn the system

INTERNAL BRAND

- Map internal stakeholder ecosystem (more in Chapter 3).
- Learn existing data, tools and skills.
- Deliver a quick-win insight through storytelling.
- Define visual identity with internal comms.

EXTERNAL BRAND

- Follow thought leaders, join PA communities, connect online with peers.
- Subscribe to quality newsletters to stay in the know.
- Understand the professional landscape through industry bodies, associations, events and community membership.

PERSONAL BRAND

- Draft a personal brand statement.
- Ask for informal feedback to identify what people value the most about you.

- Learn about personal branding through tools like LinkedIn, GitHub etc.

Weeks 5 to 8: Build visibility and expand engagement

INTERNAL BRAND

- Join key leadership meetings for a quick slot on PA.
- Run an interactive data literacy activity.
- Create an informal internal data community.
- Build relationships with internal influencers.
- Deliver high-quality insights via visuals and headlines that capture attention.

EXTERNAL BRAND

- Share case studies in your organization with your wider external network.
- Engage with external networks through thoughtful comments.
- Share data literacy progress in external forums.
- Create an event calendar that marks major industry events that you can attend.

PERSONAL BRAND

- Post a learning reflection on LinkedIn.
- Ensure LinkedIn and bios reflect the brand.
- Define two to three content themes.
- Seek out and join at least one community.
- Attend an industry event as an observer.

Weeks 9 to 12: Deepen influence and demonstrate impact

INTERNAL BRAND

- Deliver a high-quality insight product.
- Build sponsorship with senior leaders.

- Share findings at leadership forums.
- Launch newsletter or insight recap.
- Plan and host internals sessions (lunch & learn, Q&A).

EXTERNAL BRAND

- Share a case-study or lessons-learned post.
- Connect with one or two external influencers about a future speaking opportunity at your organization.
- Come up with the award goals and nomination plan with your team.

PERSONAL BRAND

- Offer value (mentoring, pro bono virtual workshop).
- Revisit and refine your brand statement.
- Write a post to mark your progress (e.g. what I learned in 90 days).

EXERCISE

What impact can you have over the next 90 days (whether it's your first 90 days or not)? Put together your own 90-day plan for how you will strengthen your internal, external and personal brand.

CHAPTER SUMMARY

- By focusing on your internal, external and personal brands, you can shape how internal and external stakeholders, customers and partners perceive you and your function.
- Building a strong PA brand requires an understanding of who holds different kinds of power and persuading people to focus their attention on you.
- Thinking in systems rather than isolated silos enables you to understand how different parts of an organization interact and

influence each other, spotting issues early and influencing how the system operates to create beneficial outcomes.

- Building a strong brand within a system relies on changing mindsets and narratives, as well as processes. PA is uniquely positioned to change organizational mindsets around issues such as data literacy and governance.

REVIEW QUESTIONS

1 What are the different types of branding for people analytics? List three strategies for building each type.

2 How will building a dashboard be seen differently with a systems-thinking lens and without a systems-thinking lens?

3 What's a good example project where you can integrate systems-thinking theory and branding skills to create impact for people analytics?

Endnotes

1 Kotler, P and Keller, K L (2016) *Marketing Management*, 15th edn, Pearson Education

2 Meadows, D H (2008) *Thinking in Systems: A Primer*, Chelsea Green Publishing

3 Qualtrics (2022) Brand Trust: What It Is and Why It's Important, Qualtrics, https://www.qualtrics.com/experience-management/brand/brand-trust/ (archived at https://perma.cc/FZ83-YU3U)

4 Wired (2002) Apple: It's All About the Brand, *Wired*, https://www.wired.com/2002/12/apple-its-all-about-the-brand/ (archived at https://perma.cc/N4RR-TNQ2)

5 Wikipedia (2025) Marketing of Apple Inc, Wikipedia, https://en.wikipedia.org/wiki/Marketing_of_Apple_Inc (archived at https://perma.cc/9SXJ-5L5X)

6 Aaker, D A (1996) *Building Strong Brands*, Free Press

7   Amabile, T M (1996) *Creativity In Context: Update to the Social Psychology Of Creativity*, 1st ed, Routledge, https://doi.org/10.4324/9780429501234 (archived at https://perma.cc/34WR-YS7W)

8   Polzer, J T and Hull, O (2018) People Analytics at McKinsey, Harvard Business School Publishing, revised January 2020, https://www.hbs.edu/faculty/Pages/item.aspx?num=53812 (archived at https://perma.cc/Q7FJ-P7BY)

9   CIPD (2018) People Analytics: Driving Business Performance with People Data, Chartered Institute of Personnel and Development, https://www.cipd.org/globalassets/media/knowledge/knowledge-hub/reports/people-analytics-us-focus_2018_tcm18-47588.pdf (archived at https://perma.cc/E3E8-DZNY)

10 Kahneman, D (2011) *Thinking, Fast and Slow*, Farrar, Straus and Giroux

11 Posner, M I and Snyder, C R R (2004) Attention and Cognitive Control. In D A Balota and E J Marsh (eds), *Cognitive Psychology: Key Readings*, Psychology Press, 205–23

12 Broadbent, D E (1958) *Perception and Communication*, Pergamon Press

13 Kram, K E (1985) *Mentoring at Work: Developmental Relationships in Organizational Life*, Scott Foresman

14 Baumeister, R F and Vohs, K D (2012) Self-Regulation and the Executive Function of the Self. In Leary, M R and Tangney, J P (eds), *Handbook of Self and Identity* (2nd ed), The Guilford Press, 180–97

15 Cialdini, R B (2007) *Influence: The Psychology of Persuasion*, Harper Collins

16 Montoya, P (2002) *The Personal Branding Phenomenon: Realizing the Power of You*, Personal Branding Press

17 Deloitte (2023) Unlocking the Value: People Analytics Maturity, India 2023, Deloitte India, https://www.contentree.com/white-papers/people-analytics-maturity-report-unlocking-the-value_414838 (archived at https://perma.cc/4TFA-DNXY)

18 Senge, P M (1990) *The Fifth Discipline: The Art and Practice of the Learning Organization*, Doubleday

19 Kotter, J P (1996) *Leading Change*, Harvard Business Review Press

20 Nadella, S (2017) *Hit Refresh: The Quest to Rediscover Microsoft's Soul and Imagine a Better Future for Everyone*, HarperBusiness

21 Tichy, N M (2002) *The Leadership Engine: How Winning Companies Build Leaders at Every Level*, HarperBusiness

22 Kitroeff, N, Gelles, D and Nicas, J (2019) The Roots of Boeing's 737 MAX Crisis: A Regulator Relaxes Its Oversight, *The New York Times*, 27 July, https://www.nytimes.com/2019/07/27/business/boeing-737-max-faa.html (archived at https://perma.cc/4TFA-DNXY)

23 Paul, R and Elder, L (2014) *Critical Thinking: Tools for Taking Charge of Your Professional and Personal Life*, 3rd edn, Pearson

24 Senge, P M (1994) *The Fifth Discipline Fieldbook: Strategies and Tools for Building a Learning Organization*, Crown

25 Meadows, D H (2008) *Thinking in Systems: A Primer*, Chelsea Green Publishing

26 Checkland, P (1999) *Systems Thinking, Systems Practice: A Methodology for Learning and Action*, Wiley

27 Cannon, W B (1932) *The Wisdom of the Body*, W W Norton & Company

28 Checkland, P (1999) *Systems Thinking, Systems Practice: A Methodology for Learning and Action*, Wiley

29 Checkland, P (1999) *Systems Thinking, Systems Practice: A Methodology for Learning and Action*, Wiley

30 Gladwell, M (2019) *Talking to Strangers: What We Should Know About the People We Don't Know*, Allen Lane

31 Meadows, D H (2008) *Thinking in Systems: A Primer*, Chelsea Green Publishing

32 Artime, O and De Domenico, M (2022) From the Origin of Life to Pandemics: Emergent Phenomena in Complex Systems, arXiv, https://arxiv.org/abs/2205.11595 (archived at https://perma.cc/52R3-MF2A)

33 Corning, P A (2002) The Re-emergence of 'Emergence': A Venerable Concept in Search of a Theory, *Complexity*, 7(6), 18–30, doi.org/10.1002/cplx.10043 (archived at https://perma.cc/4QM6-YHPV)

34 Hadnagy, C (2018) *Social Engineering: The Science of Human Hacking*, Wiley

35 Meadows, D H (2008) *Thinking in Systems: A Primer*, Chelsea Green Publishing

36 Senge, P M (2006) *The Fifth Discipline: The Art and Practice of the Learning Organization*, Doubleday

CHAPTER THREE

Building relationships in people analytics

Introduction

Existing PA courses and certification programmes tend to focus on technical competencies such as data analysis, statistical models and modelling techniques. People skills such as relationship building and stakeholder management are rarely highlighted as key skills. The same is true in the workplace. Despite frequent discussions about the importance of building good relationships with stakeholders, most organizations lack comprehensive training programmes that teach professionals how to do this. Instead, they treat it as an unspoken expectation, rather than a skill you can obtain through learning. This unspoken expectation then becomes justification to biased decisions against minority groups. This chapter is here to change that.

I want to teach you the unspoken expectations of relationship building so you can master the skills that no one explicitly trains you for and everyone assumes you should know. We start with the importance of building great relationships, giving an example of how two PA professionals' approaches to relationship management can result in very different outcomes. Next, we look at the importance of managing our energy to maintain a consistent focus, especially when working with key stakehold-ers. We then turn to creating a stakeholder map – identifying key players and understanding their influence and importance. We end the chapter by looking at managing relationships with stakeholders, with a particular focus on building trust.

LEARNING OBJECTIVES

By the end of this chapter, you will be able to:

- Articulate why building great relationships with stakeholders is vital to success.
- Understand your energy.
- Identify key players and build a stakeholder map.
- Understand and manage key players.
- Build trust with key players.

The importance of building good relationships

While technical expertise is crucial to succeeding in a PA role, developing people skills, particularly those needed to build and maintain relationships, is often underrepresented in resources and formal training. Many PA professionals express that they often have to find out how important people skills are 'the hard way'. In Chapter 1, we discussed several reasons why technical skills are often overvalued. Here, let's briefly consider why people skills are so undertaught. Two vital factors could play a role: quan-tification bias and the assumption that people skills are innate.

Quantification bias refers to the tendency to prioritize quan-tifiable data over qualitative aspects that are harder to measure.[1] In the context of professional training, this bias leads to an over-focus on technical competencies such as data analysis, pro-gramming or dashboard building, which are easier to assess than 'softer' skills such as relationship building.

There can also be an assumption that we are born with people skills and that they cannot be learned and practised. This belief can be self-limiting and have a 'glass ceiling' effect on individuals who don't believe they naturally possess people skills due to external reinforcing conditioning.[2] Educational institutions and organizations may underinvest in developing these skills because they assume they will 'come naturally' through experience or personal development outside of work (e.g. schools). However, research from Reuters suggests people skills can be developed through targeted training and practice, and neglecting this aspect of professional development can hinder career progression and organizational effectiveness.[3]

The stories of two PA professionals

Jim and Lia work at different companies. They both have about two years' experience in PA, and their latest research draws similar conclusions: employees aren't leaving their companies because of pay, workload or dissatisfaction with leadership, they are leaving because they can't see a future for themselves within their organizations.

The story from both organizations' data is clear. Teams with the lowest internal mobility have the highest turnover. Exit interviews provide supporting evidence that employees aren't chasing higher salaries or trendy perks, they are chasing confidence in their future.

Both Jim and Lia build and present the story backed by hard numbers. However, when they bring their findings to leadership, they are met with completely different responses.

Jim steps into the boardroom alongside the Chief People Officer (CPO), who has sponsored his research. The executives flick through the printed decks as he introduces the findings, laying out the problem's urgency.

Jim reinforces the data, walking them through the correlation between career stagnation and employee turnover. At first, everyone seems to be listening attentively. Some people nod. Then the questions come.

'Are we sure this isn't just a market trend?' the COO asks, his voice neutral but sceptical.

'Do we have data on how our competitors are handling this?' the CFO adds. Before Jim can answer, the CEO asks, 'Could this be part of a broader post-pandemic shift?'

The CPO responds by reiterating the data. Jim follows up with calculation methodology, attempting to reinforce the validity of their findings. But the conversation has shifted. Instead of discussing solutions, leadership is focused on validation.

The COO leans back and flips through the report again. The CFO exhales, setting his pen down. The CEO glances at the clock.

'I think we need more certainty before making any big decisions', the CFO says finally.

'Let's validate this further', the CEO adds. 'Jim, can you please go through the numbers again? I want to see more information adjusted for Covid'.

The conversation stalls as the discussion moves away from action and into more analysis, more meetings and more debate.

As Jim packs up his laptop, he catches a glimpse of the CPO's subtle disappointment. They had given leadership the data, but not enough to win them over.

Meanwhile, at a company nearby, Lia walks into the boardroom with her CPO and starts sharing the same findings and recommendations.

The CPO gets straight to the point: 'We have an internal mobility issue, and it's negatively impacting our retention. I've brought Lia, who has some insights she can share on this.'

Lia presents the key findings. The CFO nods slightly as he reviews the deck. The COO, arms crossed, studies the data. The CEO, fingers tapping on the table, leans forward.

'This makes complete sense', the CPO continues. 'We've seen this happening in the business, this just validates it.'

The CFO seems intrigued, and she starts going through the slides again. The COO, who had initially sat back with folded arms, now leans in.

'I agree', the CFO says. 'What will it take to fix this?'

The CPO turns to the COO. 'We'll need operational support to make internal mobility easier. What's your take?'

The COO responds, 'We can do it, but managers won't like losing top performers to other teams.'

Lia jumps in, 'That's exactly the issue. The data shows that if employees don't see a future here, they don't move internally, they leave altogether.'

The COO pauses for a minute and finally speaks 'Alright. But we need structure and change management support from the People function. If we just tell managers to be more flexible, it won't work.'

The CPO smiles. 'That's why we've mapped out a plan to support. Lia and I have outlined some options, targeting areas of concern according to the retention heatmap Lia prepared.'

The CEO nods. 'Let's not wait. What do we need to do first?'

Within minutes, the executive team begins budget discussions and outlines action plans. No one questions whether the data is right, only how they should act on it. By the time Lia leaves the room, execution is already in motion.

So, why did the same analysis result in two completely different outcomes? Jim and Lia had both done excellent work. Their analysis was equally compelling. But their approaches had been fundamentally different from the get-go.

Jim had focused on delivering flawless reports and well-structured presentations. He worked closely with the CPO but had had little direct engagement with other senior leaders.

Lia, however, built relationships before she stepped into the boardroom. Two weeks before the meeting, she ran into the CFO by chance in the hallway. He was checking his phone, waiting for an elevator.

'Hey, I saw you shared the year-end numbers in the town hall last week, must have been some intense work for the team on the year-end reporting', she said, smiling.

The CFO looked up, slightly surprised. 'Ah, thanks. That one was a nightmare; it took my team three days to sort it out.'

'Yeah, finance only gets noticed when something goes wrong', she joked.

He chuckled. As the elevator doors opened, she added, 'By the way, we're seeing something interesting in retention data. Career growth is showing up as a major driver of attrition – I think you'll find it relevant.'

'Huh', he said, stepping inside. 'That's worth a look. Keep me posted.'

A few days before the meeting, Lia met with the COO to discuss workforce planning. After the meeting, as Lia was packing up, the COO stretched back in his chair, rubbing his eyes and sighed, 'That was intense.'

Lia responded, 'Yeah, workforce planning is always tough. But your point about the internal movement was interesting. We're seeing employees pushing for it in the data.'

The COO looked at her and said, 'You've got numbers on that?'

'Yeah. I can walk you through some early findings if you're interested.'

'I'd like that', he said, standing. 'Managers always complain about losing good people. I'd rather keep them in-house than lose them to competitors.'

By the time Lia entered that boardroom, she wasn't presenting a cold report. She was confirming something leadership was already thinking about.

So, when Jim and the CPO presented, their analysis was something to be debated. When Lia and the CPO presented, their analysis was something to act on. The data was the same. The trust was not.

In the next section, we'll explore how to develop trusted relationships in an organization. We'll cover how to identify, understand and manage stakeholders, communicate in a way that resonates and build lasting relationships. Because at the end of the day, great data alone isn't enough – it's trust that drives change.

STOP AND THINK

Consider the key differences between how Jim and Lia presented their data. What influenced their choices? What outcomes did their methods lead to? Reflect on three key dimensions:

1   Systems thinking: How aware were they of the broader context and the interconnections influencing their audience and message?

2   Agility: How quickly and effectively did they adapt their approach in response to the situation?

3   Perception of their own power: Did they see themselves as data messengers, or as partners shaping outcomes?

Now consider these dimensions in relation to a recent experience you've had of presenting data. Could you have done anything better? How might these dimensions shape how you share insights in the future?

Understand your energy

Many PA professionals look outwards to perfect their craft (e.g. technical competencies) or use different communication tactics to impress stakeholders. Jim's story tells us that packing a presentation with advanced analysis and speaking confidently about your findings isn't enough to gain trust and credibility. Bulletproof analysis isn't enough to win people over if you come across as inauthentic and disconnected from your audience. Communication techniques and technical skills are only effective when you know yourself and, crucially, how to manage your energy.[4]

Why is energy management important?

Our energy levels can influence the way we think, speak and interact with others in very subtle ways.[5] People's instincts help them identify your energy levels, presence and authenticity.[6] In this section, we explore the importance of energy management and learn energy management tips to give you confidence and clarity and, ultimately, improve the quality of your work and insights.

One of the biggest misconceptions about productivity is that it is about time management. Many people assume that the more hours they work, the more they will achieve.[7] But the reality is that time is fixed, whereas energy fluctuates. You could have eight hours available, but if your energy level and mental clarity are low, those hours will be less effective than four hours of focused work. Energy management can be the differentiator between those who perform at a consistently high level and those who struggle with decision fatigue and burnout.

Energy levels need to be managed strategically. Willpower is not an infinite force,[8] and studies in cognitive science have shown that self-control, decision-making and focus all rely on the same limited cognitive energy pool.[9] Every decision you make consumes energy. If you've already made numerous decisions by midday, decision fatigue will start to set in, leading to shortcuts, impulsive thinking and potentially compromised analytical accuracy.

Best-in-class professionals do not just work harder; they work smarter. They own their energy reserve and use it efficiently, resting and replenishing it when necessary.

Energy management strategies

Self-awareness is the foundation of energy management. Try to start noticing what times of day you feel at your best and when you struggle. What drains you? What energizes you? Most importantly, do you structure your day according to your fluctuating energy levels? Start to track patterns. When are your most productive hours for analysis? Does your brain need to reset after long periods of focused thinking? What happens if you don't rest? By asking yourself these questions, you can start to take control of your days instead of feeling controlled by whatever's left in your tank.

Strategic energy management requires thinking about energy at cognitive, emotional and physical levels:

- Cognitive energy – group your work into clear blocks. Work out when your highest energy hours are in the day and save them for deep analytical work. Leave admin and routine low-importance tasks for times when your brain is less likely to work at full capacity.
- Emotional energy – PA professionals often deal with sensitive issues like redundancies, grievances and performance review outcomes. Imagine seeing a close work colleague's name on the redundancies list, how would you feel? To manage the emotional energy drain, try to acknowledge and honour your emotions while shifting your focus to decisions within your control. Also, be kind to yourself and beware of self-criticism. Beating yourself up about projects that are not going to plan, whether for reasons within your control or not, can be a huge drain of emotional energy. Practise self-compassion by acknowledging progress and letting go of perfectionism. If things become hard, take a short break, reset and ease yourself back in with something engaging, not overwhelming.
- Physical energy – build a healthy sleep schedule, stay hydrated and practise regular breathing exercises. It makes a huge difference to performance and mental sharpness. A five-minute 'deskercize' or short walk can help you regain focus.

With self-awareness and appropriate attention to your cognitive, emotional and physical energy, you might find your attitude towards work transitions from a sprint to a marathon and that you can consistently operate on your A game. You will also find your stakeholders starting to become easier to manage.

STOP AND THINK

Which type of energy do you most need to manage – cognitive, emotional or physical? Write down five things you could do to manage your energy better.

How to identify key players

This section provides a tried and tested guide to identifying the key players who can influence your projects and initiatives over the short and long term. This not only helps your projects succeed, but it can help your career, too. We look at a stakeholder identification method which can be adopted in many different contexts, so it's important to understand the boundaries of application (refer to Chapter 2 for more on boundary identification). You can apply this to a project, programme (consisting of multiple projects over time) or role. There are four steps:

1 Determine your purpose.
2 Brainstorm stakeholders.
3 Rate and group your stakeholders.
4 Create your stakeholder map.

Determine your purpose

Ask yourself, 'What's my goal in completing this exercise?' and think in both organizational and personal terms. Organizational goals could include:

• Building a PA capability.
• Ensuring all HR business partners (HRBP) are data literate.
• Implement a PA solution to reduce manual effort by X per cent.

Personal goals could include:

- Lead a PA project end-to-end.
- Become a go-to expert in the business on PA.
- Become a thought leader in the PA community.

Use your goals to guide you. If you get lost or distracted, return to them and ask yourself 'Is what I'm spending time on working positively towards my goals?'. If it is, carry on. If not, try to redirect your energy away from the distracting items.

STOP AND THINK

Reflect on one of your current projects or initiatives. Do you have a clear idea of what you're hoping to achieve at an organizational and personal level? Take a few minutes to write down your top three organizational and personal goals.

Brainstorm stakeholders

According to the consultancy IDEO, brainstorming is a semi-structured, team-based method of rapid idea generation.[10] One way to complete this exercise is you and a partner (if you can find one) get together and come up with a list of all relevant stakeholders for your objectives. To aid you with the brainstorming process, ask yourself the following questions:

- Who will be impacted by my work?
- Who has the power to influence my success?
- Who could prevent me from achieving my professional and personal goals?

You can then further classify your stakeholders into two groups:

- Internal stakeholders – people within your organization who have a vested interest in what you are trying to achieve; examples are the HRBP team, finance team, customer experience teams and executives.

- External stakeholders – people outside the organization who may have a vested interest in what you are trying to achieve; examples are customers, regulatory/industry bodies, suppliers and industry networks.

TOP TIP
Leverage the power of your colleagues

Don't try to do this alone. A well-connected colleague with a long tenure at the organization can sometimes be your best brainstorming partner and may be able to help you identify hidden stakeholders. They will have seen the ups and downs, the integration and separation of teams, and those who lasted and didn't last. These individuals are key to helping you navigate the complex stakeholder landscape and finding the path of least resistance.

Rate and group your stakeholders

For each stakeholder, ask the following three questions:

Grouping Question 1: Can they make or break your goal?

- Rate from 1 to 10 (1 = No impact, 10 = Absolutely critical to success or failure).

Grouping Question 2: What's your current relationship with this stakeholder?

- Rate from 1 to 10 (1 = No relationship, 10 = Strong and trusted connection).

Grouping Question 3: What is their level of influence within their environments?

- Rate from 1 to 10 (1 = Low influence, 10 = Highly influential).
- To help you determine this, you can ask yourself and your colleagues the following questions:

- Do people often seek their approval before making decisions? If they do, give a higher rating.
- Do they act as a connector, influencing multiple areas of the business? If they do, give a higher rating.

Once you've answered these three questions, set up an Excel sheet with one column for each of the ratings like the one shown in Table 3.1. Record the ratings for each stakeholder identified. It's important to review the entire list after drafting the table, as your ratings may adjust relatively based on comparisons between stakeholders.

Create your stakeholder map

This is the final step of the identification process. Create a two-by-two grid like the one shown in the bottom left-hand corner of Figure 3.1. The grid should show four quadrants, with the horizontal access representing the degree to which a stakeholder can make or break your goals. The vertical axis represents how strong your current relationship is with them, from low to high.

Map each stakeholder on the grid using their scores for the column 'Can make break goals' (for horizontal axis) and 'Current relationship level' (for vertical axis). For the horizontal axis, if the score is low, position them lower in the chart, if the score is high, position the dot higher in the chart. For the

TABLE 3.1   How to rate and group your stakeholders

Stakeholder name	Role	Can make or break goal (1–10)	Current Relationship level (1–10)	Level of influence (1–10)
Jane Woo	HRBP	8	6	9
John Garden	CFO	10	4	10

vertical axis, if the score is low, position them on the left of the chart, if the score is high, position them on the right of the chart.

Now you have all relevant stakeholders mapped as dots, you can represent each individual's level of influence through the size of their dot. A stakeholder with higher influence over their environment would be a larger circle.

As a bonus step, you could add further detail to the map, but note that this adds complexity and may make it hard for others to understand:

- Use colour coding to show types of stakeholders, for example, blue for internal stakeholders and green for external stakeholders.
- Use lines to connect the stakeholders and show their relationship with each other. Thicker lines can represent tighter relationships, and thinner lines can represent looser relationships.

EXERCISE

Consider one of your current goals (perhaps one that you came up with in the previous exercise). Create a stakeholder map for this goal.

Understanding and managing key players

Now that you have a stakeholder map, it is time to integrate managing your energy and the stakeholders you work with. To achieve your personal and professional goals, you want to maximize your energy efficiency and navigate through the map with a path of the least resistance. This section will teach you how.

Firstly, determine the priority stakeholders you want to focus most of your energies on. As you complete this exercise, be careful not to overlook hidden influencers – those who don't have a

FIGURE 3.1   The stakeholder identification, analysis and engagement process

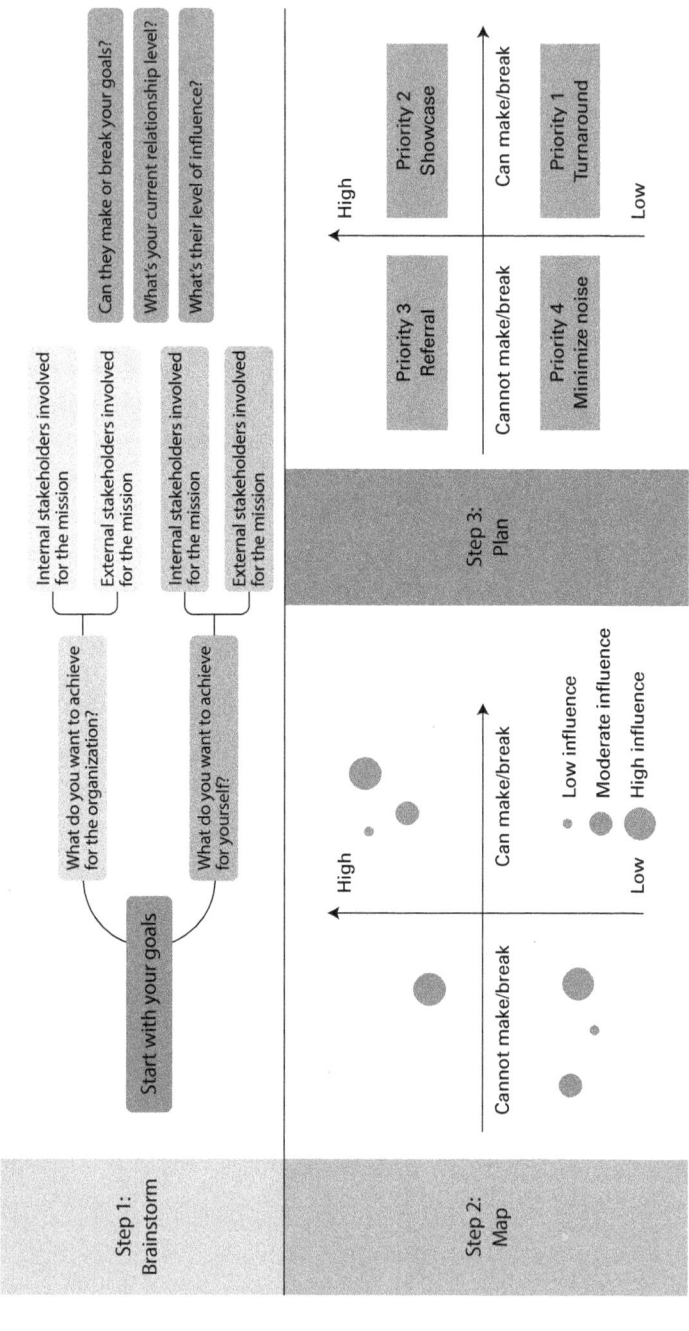

big title but have a big voice. Return to your stakeholder map. There are four quadrants:

- Bottom right – These stakeholders are key decision-makers who you have a weak relationship with but who can make or break your initiative.

    - *Strategy:* Turnaround.

    - *Priority:* Highest priority. These stakeholders' decisions could make or break your initiative. Focus your energy on engaging these stakeholders and gaining their trust. For turnaround efforts, focus on the high-influence stakeholders in the quadrants who are closer to the bottom-right corner first, then move on to others.

- Top right – The stakeholders in this region are your key allies. You have a good to great relationship with them, and they have a significant impact on the make or break of your initiative. Ideally, your initiative sponsor should sit on the top right, if not, it's time to get to work.

    - *Strategy:* Showcase.

    - *Priority:* Second highest priority. Don't be complacent about these stakeholders simply because they are supportive. You need to harness the momentum of this group to keep them engaged and satisfied and ensure you have strong backing. Leverage this group's amplification power, particularly the larger dots who can be your biggest advocates with their network and help you build your brand.

- Top left – The stakeholders in this region are your friends, you have a good to great relationship with them, but they don't have too much decision-making power on your initiative.

    - *Strategy:* Referral.

    - *Priority:* Third highest priority, the stakeholders in this quadrant have high trust in you and they speak highly of you and the initiative. While they don't have a direct impact on the success or failure of this initiative, they can connect you to stakeholders you may want to turn around or sing your praises to the right people at the right moment. These stakeholders will happily do you a favour because of the trust you've already built. They can also act as the key mediator if an issue arises with a stakeholder in the turnaround quadrant due to their lack of decision-making power in your initiative.

- Bottom left – The stakeholders in this region have weaker relationships with you. They are not critical to you achieving your goals and their decisions cannot make or break your project.
  - *Strategy:* Minimize noise.
  - *Priority:* Lowest priority. While most might have good intentions, be aware of harmful noise from this group that saps your energy. Think of them as internet 'trolls'. In real life, this group might consist of people unwilling to change and who also cannot influence the change decision. They might constantly make you doubt yourself and your worth through passive-aggressive comments etc.

Organizations rarely stay the same, and neither should your approach to managing stakeholders. Stakeholder management is not a one-time task; it is a continuous and evolving process. The map you create today will not be the same one you need in six months. As your project progresses, priorities shift, relationships change and new stakeholders emerge. Regularly reassess who your most critical stakeholders are, how their level of influence may have changed and whether new relationships need to be developed.

> **TOP TIP**
> Assess your options
>
> There are many ways to map stakeholders. Try a simple Google image search to discover an array of options. As you gain more experience in PA, you may want to tailor the approach set out in this chapter to your style of working.

Now that you have a prioritized view of your stakeholders and a rough understanding of the key players, it's time to learn how you can manage each type of key player.

Building trust with key players

You have now identified your stakeholders, analysed them and have a good understanding of who should get the most priority and energy. So how will you build trusted relationships with them? This section explores how PA professionals can build strong relationships with stakeholders by focusing on human-centred design, credibility, communication and personalized service.

What is trust?

To build trust, it's important to understand its key components. Francis Frei from Harvard Business School gives a robust framework for trust, suggesting it is built on the foundation of three key elements: empathy, logic and authenticity.[11] When people perceive that you truly care about them, your reasoning is sound and you are being your genuine self, trust forms naturally. Conversely, a breakdown in any of these areas can erode trust. Frei highlights that people often lose trust not because all three are missing but because one is consistently compromised.[12]

EMPATHY – WHAT'S IN IT FOR ME?

Let's begin with the empathy pillar. One of the most effective ways to build trust through empathy is to understand your stakeholder's motivations. People are far more likely to support your initiative if they see how it benefits them. This is where the 'What's in it for me?' (WIIFM) principle comes in, ensuring that your insights are not just technically sound but also relevant and meaningful to those who use them. Asking the WIIFM question challenges you to think from the stakeholder's perspective.

> **WIIFM principle**: a way of looking at initiatives from your stakeholders' perspectives, considering how it benefits them.

Different stakeholders have different priorities. A senior executive may care about HR risks, an HRBP may care about the management effectiveness and a CPO may care about the effectiveness of current HR technologies and systems. This is where human-centred design (HCD), which we discussed in Chapter 1, becomes very important. HCD encourages you to step into your stakeholders' shoes, deeply understanding their pain points, goals and daily realities before presenting data. Rather than assuming what matters to them, you engage in active listening, co-creation and iterative problem-solving to ensure that your solutions address a real problem.

To apply WIIFM, begin with listening sessions (more on listening in Chapter 6) at the start of your project to understand the WIIFM for each key player. Throughout the project, involve the key players through a 'partner lens', instead of treating them as silent consumers of your progress update. This way, you will have buy-in, trust and impact from the get-go.

LOGIC – PERSONAL COMMUNICATION STYLES

Communicating work to different stakeholders can result in varied results, even if the analysis and methodology are the same. Understanding personal styles can allow you to adapt your approach and build trust more effectively.

Personal communication styles describe how individuals prefer to interact, process information and make decisions.[13] Each style has its expectations around how logic should be structured and delivered. If your communication style doesn't align with your stakeholder's style, even strong ideas can feel confusing or unconvincing. It's not that the logic is flawed, but it isn't delivered in a way that resonates. In short, the perception of your logic is shaped not just by what you say, but by *how* you say it.

So, how can you determine someone's style? You can observe what they focus on in conversations and how they interact with others. There are two key dimensions to pay attention to:

1   Do they value relationships or task completion more?
    Stakeholders who prioritize relationships tend to be more people-focused, valuing team dynamics, collaboration and harmony. Stakeholders who prioritize task completion focus on efficiency, productivity and getting things done.
2   Do they tend to ask or tell?
    Some stakeholders prefer to ask questions and seek input before making decisions. Others prefer to assert their views without much discussion.

By combining these two dimensions, you can classify stakeholders into one of four communication styles as shown in Table 3.2. Leverage the strategies in the table to personalize trust-building approaches. Recognizing and adapting to different personal styles will help you retain authenticity while communicating effectively to build trust.

AUTHENTICITY – MINIMIZE INFORMATION ASYMMETRY

Information asymmetry occurs when one party possesses more or better information than the other, often resulting in imbalances in decision-making and trust.[14] In workplace settings, this

TABLE 3.2 Strategies for the four communication styles

Personal communication styles	How to build trust	Best communication style	Key focus	Avoid
Amiable (relationship-oriented, asks for input)	Start with personal connections, be warm and approachable.	Collaborative and reassuring, allowing space for discussion.	Show how your work supports team success and harmony.	Being too direct or dismissing their need for group input.
Expressive (relationship-oriented, tells)	Be enthusiastic and engaging, share your vision.	High-energy, big-picture discussions that inspire.	Highlight future impact and creative possibilities.	Overloading them with too many details or rigid structures.
Analytic (task-oriented, asks for input)	Provide data, structure, and logical reasoning.	Detail-oriented, methodical and fact-driven.	Show them how and why your approach is valid, backed by evidence.	Being vague, emotional or rushing decisions.
Driver (task-oriented, tells)	Be concise, confident and results-driven.	Direct, to-the-point, and action-focused.	Present solutions, outcomes and efficiencies.	Rambling, unnecessary details, or indecisiveness.

SOURCE Adapted from Merrill and Reid (1981), this table reinterprets core ideas from *Personal Styles and Effective Performance* to illustrate key personal style distinctions and strategies to manage each.

gap can be created by one party withholding information, which is often done with good intentions. For example, you may be trying to prevent someone from getting hurt (from your perspective), so you omit information that might help their development. When you create information asymmetry, it damages your authenticity.

This is where we integrate energy management with trust. Our goal is to minimize energy expenditure and maximize outcomes. In an environment where information asymmetry is high and trust is low, information travels slowly and people can feel like they need to spend extra cognitive and emotional energy to 'read between the lines' or 'figure someone out' to understand intent.

When people feel like they can predict your reactions and behaviour, they feel safer engaging with you.[15] When you conceal information, behave inconsistently, or appear over-rehearsed or performative, you risk damaging your authenticity and trust. That's why transparency in interactions is so important. Being transparent means:

- Facilitating and encouraging open conversations, rather than insisting on 'what the data says' and 'based on the analysis'.
- Showing how you arrived at the insights, and outlining the assumptions and limitations of your insights.
- Owning mistakes and uncertainties. No data is perfect. If there are gaps, acknowledge them rather than overpromise or make vague statements to sound confident.

Ultimately, authenticity ensures that PA is seen as a trusted business function rather than just a service provider. For more models and techniques you can use to build trust and foster strong relationships, see Chapter 6.

TOP TIP
Be honest about what you don't know

Early career professionals may be reluctant to admit uncertainties in case it undermines their credibility, but the longer-term impact of not admitting uncertainties can be worse than losing credibility in the moment. Showing vulnerability allows you to connect with others at a human level. Instead of overselling certainty, invite discussions, share potential risks and show how insights can evolve.

CHAPTER SUMMARY

- Presenting data alone is unlikely to result in stakeholder buy-in. Building trust-fuelled relationships with key players will give your initiatives the best chance of success.

- Managing your cognitive, emotional and physical energy will make stakeholder management far easier, and even enjoyable. It's difficult to build great relationships if you are depleted cognitively, emotionally and physically.

- Creating a stakeholder map can help you easily identify which individuals need most of your energy.

- Adopt one of four strategies to manage your stakeholders, depending on where they appear on your stakeholder map: 'turnaround', 'showcase', 'referral' or 'minimize noise'.

- Focus on building trusted relationships with stakeholders by using the three-pillar framework for building trust: empathy, logic and authenticity.

REVIEW QUESTIONS

1 How do you plan to manage your energy?

2 How has reading this chapter changed your perception of PA?

3 How will you map your stakeholders for your next goal?

Endnotes

1 Janesky, L (2019) Quantification Bias, Think Daily, https://www.
   thinkdaily.com/2019/05/quantification-bias/ (archived at
   https://perma.cc/2LVS-PCVG)
2 Correll, S J and Ridgeway, C L (2003) Expectation States Theory, in
   J Delamater (ed) *Handbook of Social Psychology*, Springer, 29–51
3 Balch, O (2025) Brand Watch: Why Investing in 'Soft' Skills Makes
   Hard-headed Business Sense, Reuters, 24 February, www.reuters.
   com/sustainability/boards-policy-regulation/brand-watch-why-
   investing-soft-skills-makes-hard-headed-business-sense-2025-02-24/
   (archived at https://perma.cc/CHF8-HWT6)
4 Antonopoulou, H (2024) The Value of Emotional Intelligence:
   Self-Awareness, Self-Regulation, Motivation and Empathy as Key
   Components, ResearchGate, 2024, www.researchgate.net/
   publication/379764627_The_Value_of_Emotional_Intelligence_Self-
   Awareness_Self-Regulation_Motivation_and_Empathy_as_Key_
   Components (archived at https://perma.cc/T3WL-DPA9)
5 Wilson, M (2002) Six Views of Embodied Cognition, *Psychonomic
   Bulletin and Review*, 10(4), 625–36
6 Leisten, L M, Findling, F, Bellinghausen, J, Kinateder, M, Probst, T,
   Lion, D and Shiban, Y (2021) The Effect of Nonlexical Verbal
   Signals on the Perceived Authenticity, Empathy and Understanding
   of a Listener, *European Journal of Counselling Psychology*, 10(1),
   https://doi.org/10.46853/001c.27434 (archived at https://perma.cc/
   HCE8-SBFC
7 Otter.ai (2022) 5 Common Workplace Productivity Myths and
   Misconceptions Debunked, Otter.ai Blog, 15 August, www.otter.ai/
   blog/5-myths-misconceptions-about-workplace-productivity
   (archived at https://perma.cc/MM2Z-PS65)
8 Baumeister, R F, Bratslavsky, E, Muraven, M and Tice, D M (1998)
   Ego Depletion: Is the Active Self a Limited Resource? *Journal of
   Personality and Social Psychology*, 74(5), 1252–65, https://doi.org/
   10.1037/0022-3514.74.5.1252 (archived at https://perma.cc/92UZ-
   ZFUQ)
9 Muraven, M, Tice, D M and Baumeister, R F (1998) Self-Control as a
   Limited Resource: Regulatory Depletion Patterns, *Journal of
   Personality and Social Psychology*, 74(3), 774–89, https://doi.org/

10.1037/0022-3514.74.3.774 (archived at https://perma.cc/8FWK-TG64)

10 IDEO (2025) Brainstorming, IDEO Design Thinking, https://designthinking.ideo.com/resources/brainstorming (archived at https://perma.cc/Q3P2-R2UH)

11 Frei, F and Morriss, A (2021) Trust: The Foundation of Leadership, *Leader to Leader*, 99, 20–25, www.hbs.edu/faculty/Pages/item.aspx?num=59724 (archived at https://perma.cc/C8MW-25UJ)

12 Frei, F (2018) How to Build (and Rebuild) Trust, TED Talks, April, https://www.ted.com/talks/frances_frei_how_to_build_and_rebuild_trust (archived at https://perma.cc/7B8W-SBXJ)

13 Merrill, D W and Reid, R H (1981) *Personal Styles and Effective Performance*, Chilton Book Company

14 Akerlof, G A (1970) The Market for 'Lemons': Quality Uncertainty and the Market Mechanism, *Quarterly Journal of Economics*, 84(3), 488–500

15 Murray, S L, Lamarche, V, Seery, M D, Jung, H Y, Griffin, D W and Brinkman, C (2021) The Social-Safety System: Fortifying Relationships in the Face of the Unforeseeable, *Journal of Personality and Social Psychology*, 120(1), 99–130, https://doi.org/10.1037/pspi0000245 (archived at https://perma.cc/7B8W-SBXJ)

CHAPTER FOUR

Managing projects in people analytics

Introduction

So far, we have covered the importance of people skills for early career professionals, the history of PA, the foundations of systems thinking and how to identify and manage stakeholders. It is now time for us to move on to one of the more practical skills necessary to become a well-rounded PA practitioner – project management.

Project management isn't just for project managers. It's a foundational business skill, and the earlier you learn it, the more powerful it becomes, no matter what role you are in. When you are early in your career, you get handed a lot of 'projects' to work on, often without any formal teaching about how to manage them. This means that projects can be treated simply as a set of tasks with little consideration of the scope, stakeholders, risks or timelines.

Learning how to think like a project manager is one of the most impactful skills you can develop. It's an art and a science, and doing it well can completely change how you perform and how others perceive you. We begin this chapter by looking at why project management skills are so integral to you as an early career PA professional. We progress to consider different project management methodologies and applications that will be helpful for you to be aware of before looking at an extended real-world example, which uses a fictional initiative to show how different methodologies can be applied in practice. We finish by considering some of the common project management challenges you are likely to encounter.

LEARNING OBJECTIVES

By the end of this chapter, you will be able to:

- Articulate why an understanding of project management approaches is key to succeeding in a PA role.
- Describe Waterfall, Agile and hybrid project management approaches, along with their benefits and limitations.
- Apply Waterfall and Agile approaches to an HR project and pick elements of both to construct a hybrid approach.
- Deal with common PA project management challenges.

The importance of project management

Many PA roles require you to work cross-functionally and manage senior key stakeholders from day one. You quickly become the bridge between data, people and strategy, with multiple departments relying on your work. Project management helps you manage these moving pieces, communicate clearly and assertively (regardless of your title) and keep everyone aligned. It provides you with the tools to collaborate smoothly, delegate when necessary and deliver with confidence. When you manage projects well, people see you as reliable, organized and outcome-focused.

A significant portion of your work is likely to be project-based, and people-data projects are rarely straightforward. They often come with ambiguity, shifting priorities and multiple dependencies, especially when you are waiting on data you don't yet have or navigating evolving stakeholder goals. Effective project management helps you break complex problems into manageable steps, plan realistically around data-driven time-lines and remain flexible when things inevitably change.

And here is the positive side effect on your career: when you run projects effectively, you get noticed. The ability to lead with-out a manager title can set you apart. Don't wait to be promoted to show leadership. When you break down your work, drive progress and consistently deliver, you naturally earn more respon-sibility. That is how career growth happens. You build a reputation as someone who gets things done, and that is the kind of reputa-tion that leads to trust, visibility and new opportunities.

STOP AND THINK

Consider how you (and your organization) currently approach PA projects:

- Are they recognized as projects that need to be run in a specific way?
- If they are, do you follow a specific methodology and if so, how rigidly do you follow it?
- How effective do you think your current project management practices are, and what impact do they have on the PA function and organization?

Project management methodologies and applications

Think of project management as building a solid foundation for a house. You can have the best design and materials, but if the foundation is shaky, everything's at risk. There are many project management methodologies out there and specific lingo, so it is easy to get lost. In this section, we zoom in to provide you with a simplified view of the purpose and application of project management in PA. We then zoom out to show you the various methodologies out there and the relationship between them.

Project management – purpose and application

At its core, project management is about the organization and coordination of resources to get things done. A useful framework for thinking about project management is the Input-Process-Output (IPO) framework.[1] If you are asked to accomplish something, you have a collection of resources (input) that need to undergo a transformation process to achieve the desired outcome (output). As a project manager, you are responsible for ensuring that the end-to-end transformation of input into output happens according to your customers' expectations.

The following are three examples of projects you might be asked to manage.

1 Headcount reporting

   - Input: Inconsistent headcount data across various legacy systems and unclear ownership of reporting; lack of standard definitions.

   - Project management process: Working with key customer teams to align requirements and definitions (e.g. who counts as headcount) and facilitate an automated reporting process; using project management tools to structure phases, assign ownership and manage stakeholders; hosting status updates and workshops to engage stakeholders and customers.

   - Output: A live headcount report with agreed definitions, automated updates and clear ownership that will be used by HR and finance for planning and reporting.

2 New starter turnover analysis

- Input: High turnover among employees within the first six months and lack of data between core HR, finance systems and exit survey.

- Output: Findings report highlighting early attrition trends and potential drivers – used to update onboarding processes and improve early employee experience.

- Project management process: Scoping and agreeing on analysis timeline; partnering with talent acquisition, HR business partners, finance and technology teams to obtain the necessary data; linking manual exit survey and core HR data; managing data quality checks and facilitating review workshops to validate insights and agree on next steps.

3 Quarterly pulse survey analysis

- Input: Quarterly engagement surveys with limited visibility into actionable trends; concerns regarding data trust and a lack of follow-up.

- Output: Quarterly insight reports summarizing sentiment themes and drivers, linked to engagement priorities – shared with leaders and team managers to support targeted action planning.

- Project management process: Facilitating the definition and agreement on the analytical approach between data science and data consumers; collaborating timelines with HR business partners to interpret results and add commentary; building a delivery plan to ensure timely quarterly insight production and distribution; establishing feedback loops through regular check-ins and embedded findings into existing leadership rhythms.

TOP TIP

The difference between project management and project delivery

Project management involves planning, organizing and ensuring everything runs smoothly. **Project delivery** focuses on completing the actual work.

Early in your career, you are likely to manage and deliver projects. Recognizing the difference between the two roles is key to your career progression. The more you start to separate those responsibilities in your mind, the easier it becomes to step into more strategic, leadership-focused roles.

Project management methodologies

Project management may sound like a complicated process to many people, but at its core, it is something you already do every day. This section provides the foundational frameworks you need to start practising and acquiring the skills of project management.

There are many project management methodologies available, but they can be broadly categorized based on the most suitable environments in which they should be applied.

Waterfall project management: A way to manage projects sequentially and linearly where each stage of the project has to be completed before the next begins.[2] This makes any changes in these areas difficult to accommodate later, as the methodology assumes a fixed plan and relies on detailed initial documentation to guide the entire process.

Agile project management: A project management methodology that focuses on flexibility and responsiveness to real-time requirements. It manages work iteratively and incrementally, allowing teams to adapt as new requirements emerge rather than delivering the entire project output near the end.[3]

WATERFALL PROJECT MANAGEMENT

You know a project is managed using the Waterfall method when the project scope, time and cost are determined in the early phases of the lifecycle. You will probably see a detailed project plan with each stage of the project listed with the dates outlined. Budgets and timelines are rigid, strict and sequential, meaning that a delay in earlier stages of the project will delay subsequent stages of the project. It is a project manager's role to make sure each step of the project is delivered on time and budget.

- *Think of it as*: The 'perfection' method, because it assumes perfect plans, perfect timelines and perfect requirements from the start, with little room for error. Success depends hugely on 'being right'.
- *When to use*: Waterfall project management is frequently used in controlled environments where changes are not supposed to happen very often (e.g. building construction).[4]
- *Limitations*:
  - Heavy on documentation (covered later in the chapter). Time can be spent producing documents rather than tangible outcomes.
  - Rigid structure. Difficult to pivot easily and even minor changes result in mountains of paperwork.

AGILE PROJECT MANAGEMENT

You know a project is managed using the Agile method when the project scope is flexible, and work is delivered in short, iterative cycles called sprints. Instead of a fixed, detailed plan laid out from start to finish, you will likely see a prioritized backlog of tasks on a board (e.g. Kanban board) that evolves as the project progresses. Budgets and timelines are adaptive and allow for continuous feedback and change.[5] Agile projects embrace uncertainty and prioritize collaboration, meaning teams can pivot, quickly responding to new information and customer needs. It is the role of the Agile project manager (sometimes called scrum master) to ensure that the team stays focused, delivers incremental value and continuously improves.

- *Think of it as*: The 'chameleon' method, because it is extremely flexible and adapts seamlessly to changes in the external environment. By incrementally building the project output from the start, Agile enables continuous delivery of value in highly dynamic environments.

- *When to use*: Agile project management is frequently employed in rapidly changing environments where requirements are expected to evolve (e.g. software development or product innovation).

- *Limitations*:
  - Adaptable and fluid timelines mean that deadlines can slip and costs can add up.
  - Not all projects lend themselves to iteration and feedback, especially data projects.
  - Feedback can lead you the wrong way – you might begin by wanting to design a horse and end up designing a camel.

HYBRID/BALANCED PROJECT MANAGEMENT

You know a project is managed using a hybrid or balanced method when it combines elements of both traditional (Waterfall) and Agile project management. In these projects, high-level scope, time and budget are often planned upfront, similar to the Waterfall approach, but the execution may follow Agile principles – breaking work into iterative cycles, encouraging collaboration and adapting to change along the way. You will probably see a structured project roadmap, an evolving backlog and regular sprint reviews. Budgets and timelines still matter, but there is more flexibility in how teams deliver value. The project manager works closely with business stakeholders and Agile teams to balance control and adaptability.[6]

- *When to use:* hybrid project management is often the most practical approach in real-world scenarios, where certain aspects of the project require predictability (e.g. compliance or integration) while others benefit from agility (e.g. user experience or software features).

Your project is a mini system

Now, think back to what we covered in Chapter 2. Project management can take place at both a personal and organizational level. But wherever it happens, projects don't operate in isolation; they are often connected to broader objectives (e.g. a personal career shift or a company-wide programme).

The Project Management Institute (PMI) states that good project managers need to think in systems because projects don't happen on their own. They are linked to bigger goals, internal processes and sometimes external factors.[7] So, if you are getting into project management, it is helpful to see it as running a small, temporary system with lots of moving parts that all need to stay in sync to deliver results.

Let's revisit the examples we looked at earlier. The headcount reporting project might appear straightforward, but it could form part of a wider organizational initiative to digitize HR records. The new starter turnover project may be linked to a broader effort, possibly led by finance, to reduce overall costs by enhancing employee retention. Meanwhile, the pulse survey project may be just one element of a larger HR strategy refresh aimed at boosting employee engagement and shaping workplace culture.

In each case, what may seem like an isolated project is contributing to something much bigger. Viewing your project as part of a system keeps the broader context in focus, helps ensure alignment with overall goals and ultimately makes your work more impactful.

Managing projects using different approaches

In this section, we use a fictional real-world example of recruitment funnel analysis to demonstrate how to apply different project management approaches.

WHAT WOULD YOU DO?
Number 1

You are a PA specialist at Taj Motor Group. The recruitment head, who is new to the role, meets with you to discuss gaps in the recruitment data. She is concerned that leaders don't know what their conversions are like through each stage of the recruitment process, and she doesn't know where to begin when looking at process efficiencies. 'In all the places I worked for they all have a recruitment funnel which shows the volume to applications passing through each stage and it can be then sliced and diced for further questions. Is this something that you can help me to deliver?', she asks. After asking some questions, you establish the following:

- Recruitment data is not captured consistently across different departments. Some use spreadsheets; others rely on the ATS (applicant tracking system), and a few manually track outcomes via email. This inconsistency makes it difficult to gain a reliable, end-to-end view of the recruitment process.

- There is currently no shared definition of what a 'stage' is in the recruitment process. For example, some hiring managers count initial screening as a stage, while others do not. This lack of standardization creates challenges when comparing data across teams or identifying process bottlenecks.

- The recruitment head wants to build credibility with leadership by presenting clean, consistent data – ideally in a visual format that tells a clear story and enables deeper analysis. The ultimate goal is not just reporting, but using the recruitment funnel to uncover drop-off points, identify areas for improvement and drive more efficient and effective hiring decisions.

- Time is a factor – there is a quarterly leadership offsite in six weeks and she would like to present the first version of a recruitment funnel dashboard at that meeting.

- Resources for this project are modest – there is no dedicated budget, so you will need to work with existing internal tools (such as the ATS and Power BI) and collaborate with available internal teams. You may need to do some light data wrangling or design work yourself, depending on the support available from People Systems.

After conducting stakeholder identification and analysis (covered in Chapter 3), you also confirm that your stakeholders include:

- The People Systems team leader (Priority 1), who you don't know very well. They maintain the ATS and can help access and interpret raw data.

- The recruitment head (Priority 2), who is your main point of contact and project sponsor.

- Department heads (Priority 2), who will be consumers of the insights.

- HRBPs and the Recruitment team leaders (Priority 3), who can help strengthen the confidence of the department heads on the adoption of the funnel.

- Hiring managers (Priority 4), who may have differing views on how recruitment stages should be defined and tracked.

It is your job to decide which project management methodology to follow to ensure the project runs smoothly and that you complete it in time for the offsite in six weeks. Using the information in the rest of this section, decide whether a Waterfall, Agile or hybrid approach would be most suited to this project.

The Waterfall approach

This section outlines how you could run the Taj Motor Group project using the Waterfall methodology. We look at the different roles, documents and project stages.

WATERFALL PROJECT ROLES

Project manager's typical responsibilities

- Plans and oversees the full project.
- Manages scope, timeline and resources.
- Coordinates teams and handles risk.

In this case:

- Coordinates the project timeline and tracks progress.
- Engages stakeholders.
- Plans phases.
- Manages risks (e.g. data delays).

Project sponsor's typical responsibilities

- Provides strategic direction.
- Secures resources and stakeholder buy-in.
- Resolves escalated issues.

In this case (the recruitment head):

- Sets the vision.
- Champions the dashboard to leadership.
- Resolves definition disagreements.

Business analyst's typical responsibilities

- Gathers and documents business needs.
- Translates needs into functional requirements.
- Bridges users and developers.

In this case (you or someone in your role):

- Conducts interviews with stakeholders.
- Defines recruitment stages.
- Documents data requirements.

SME's typical responsibilities

- Provides deep expertise in specific areas.
- Validates the accuracy of requirements and outputs.

In this case:

- Recruitment leaders and the recruitment head offer insights on how recruitment currently works and validate funnel logic.
- HR System team members advise about system constraints and limitations.

Developer/designer's typical responsibilities

- Builds technical or visual components.
- Designs reports, dashboards or systems based on requirements.

In this case (you or a business intelligence (BI) colleague):

- Builds the Power BI dashboard.
- Cleans the data and design visuals for leadership storytelling.

Tester's typical responsibilities

- Reviews and validates deliverables.
- Confirms functionality meets expectations.
- Identifies bugs or data issues.

In this case (the recruitment head and selected department heads):

- Tests the dashboard for clarity, accuracy and usability before presentation.

Trainer's typical responsibilities

- Teaches users how to use tools or systems.
- Develops training materials and sessions.
- Ensures smooth user adoption.

In this case (you or someone from People Systems or HR):

- Runs short sessions or create quick guides to help users understand the dashboard and definitions.

User's typical responsibilities

- Consumes and interacts with the final product.
- Uses insights to make decisions or take action.
- Provides feedback.

In this case (department heads, hiring managers and leadership):

- Uses the dashboard to monitor conversions and improve recruitment efficiency.

WATERFALL PROJECT DOCUMENTATION

Waterfall project management values clarity, traceability and sign-off, and well-structured documents are necessary at each stage to avoid misalignment, scope creep or last-minute surprises. These documents can be used as 'evidence' if anything goes wrong.

> **Scope creep:** A commonly used business term to describe unplanned, expansive changes to a project's agreed original scope. It can be triggered by situations such as changes in stakeholders, the involvement of additional stakeholders or evolving business needs.

Typical essential documents project managers produce include:

- **Project charter:** A high-level document that kicks off the project. It gives a quick snapshot of why you're doing this, what you hope to achieve, what is in (and out) of scope, the timeline and who is involved.
- **Requirements document:** A detailed breakdown of what the dashboard needs to do, what data it should include and how

users will interact with it, to ensure everyone is on the same page from the start.

- **Project plan/timeline:** Often created in Excel or Microsoft Project, this shows tasks, deadlines, owners and dependencies. You will usually see this as a task list or Gantt chart – great for tracking progress.
- **Risk register:** A table of potential risks that can stop the project from being delivered on time and budget. It typically includes the nature of risk, likelihood, risk owner and risk severity (red, amber, green).
- **User acceptance testing (UAT) plan:** A list of test scenarios to ensure the dashboard works as intended and meets stakeholder expectations before final sign-off.
- **Project retrospective report:** A brief wrap-up of what was delivered, how it performed against goals and any lessons learned for future projects.

Waterfall project management tools prioritize structured planning and documentation, typically using detailed Gantt charts created in Excel or MS Project for task tracking and timelines. Documents such as project charters, requirements documents, risk registers and retrospective reports are stored centrally (e.g. SharePoint or shared cloud drive folders) to maintain clarity, traceability and control.

Dependencies: The things that need to happen before you can proceed with the next steps of the project.

Gantt chart: A chart that visualizes a project schedule over its duration, showing key dates and durations of each stage of the project. Due to its ability to visualise sequence, it's a fundamental concept for Waterfall and hybrid project environments.

WATERFALL PROJECT STAGES

Waterfall projects typically follow the following sequence:

1 Start:

- Outline the goal: develop a standardized recruitment funnel dashboard to visualize hiring efficiency and identify bottlenecks.

- Create a concise project charter summarizing the purpose, scope, timeline (six weeks) and key stakeholders, including the recruitment head, People Systems, department heads and HRBPs.

- Hold a focused kick-off meeting to ensure stakeholder alignment and approve the project charter.

2 Plan:

- Conduct a data audit with People Systems to assess existing recruitment data practices and identify gaps.

- Organize a stakeholder workshop to define and standardize recruitment stage definitions.

- Prepare a concise requirements document to outline the dashboard's functionalities, user interactions and acceptance criteria.

- Develop a comprehensive work breakdown structure (WBS), breaking the project into smaller, manageable tasks detailing activities, deliverables, deadlines, responsibilities and potential risks, which will form the basis for a detailed and actionable project plan.

3 Deliver:

- Gather and process recruitment data.

- Rapidly develop the dashboard in Power BI, integrating regular stakeholder feedback.

- Conduct lightweight internal testing aligned with the UAT plan to confirm dashboard functionality and usability before release.

4 Monitor:

- Conduct weekly checkpoint meetings.
- Track progress against the project plan.
- Proactively manage risks via a concise risk register.
- Ensure consistent communication with stakeholders.

5 Close:

- Present the completed recruitment funnel dashboard at the leadership offsite.
- Run a targeted, practical training session and concise user documentation summarizing key functions and frequently asked questions.
- Conclude with a brief project retrospective report, capturing lessons learned and recommendations for ongoing dashboard enhancements.

The Agile approach

This section outlines how you could run the Taj Motor group project using the Agile methodology. We look at the different roles, documents, ceremonies and tools, and project stages.

AGILE PROJECT ROLES

Product owner's typical responsibilities:

- Defines vision.
- Sets priorities.
- Clarifies requirements.

In this case (the recruitment head):

- Sets clear dashboard objectives/priorities and defines required functionality.

Scrum master/iteration manager's typical responsibilities

- Facilitates the team.
- Removes obstacles.
- Ensures Agile practices.

In this case (you):

- Coordinates activities.
- Resolves issues.
- Manages timeline.
- Supports stakeholder engagement.

Development team's typical responsibilities

- Delivers product increments.
- Collaborates closely to add value.

In this case (you, People Systems team, internal staff):

- Build, test and refine the recruitment funnel dashboard.

Stakeholders' typical responsibilities

- Provide feedback.
- Validate requirements.
- Ensure alignment.

In this case (department heads, HRBPs, recruitment team leaders, hiring managers):

- Provide regular input, validation and feedback to ensure the dashboard meets business needs.

Scrum master/iteration manager: A role responsible for supporting Agile teams to deliver work through making sure values are delivered iteratively and incrementally.

Sprint/iteration: A fixed period in Agile methodology, typically lasting for one to four weeks and focusing on delivering incremental value through rapid cycles of planning, delivery and feedback.

Minimum viable product (MVP): The simplest version of a product that provides immediate value and allows for iterative feedback and refinement.

JIRA: A project and issue tracking software often utilized for Agile project management. It supports various Agile methodologies, but can be perceived as 'overly technical' for beginners in Agile.

Microsoft Planner: Developed by Microsoft, this is a lightweight project and task management tool that enables team collaboration via Kanban boards. Compared to JIRA, Microsoft Planner offers a simple, user-friendly interface ideal for basic task management and team collaboration.

AGILE DOCUMENTATION, CEREMONIES AND TOOLS

Agile project management values adaptability, collaboration and continuous improvement over extensive documentation. While some documentation remains important, it must be minimal and meaningful. Regular communication, feedback and iterative improvements are the focus. Essential documents include short project summaries or user stories capturing just enough detail to clarify expectations without impacting efficiency.

Instead of extensive documentation, Agile emphasizes clear and frequent ceremonies, such as:

- **Sprint planning:** Short, collaborative meetings where the team agrees on goals, tasks and priorities for the upcoming sprint.

- **Daily stand-ups:** Brief, daily meetings where team members discuss their progress, raise obstacles and quickly align on the next steps.
- **Sprint reviews/demos:** Regular showcases allowing stakeholders to see and provide immediate feedback on incremental progress of the dashboard.
- **Sprint retrospectives:** Sessions at the end of each sprint to discuss what is and isn't working and to identify actionable improvements.

Typical Agile tools supporting these ceremonies include.

- Kanban or scrum boards (e.g. Jira, Microsoft Planner).
- Visual task-tracking tools that clearly show progress, prioritization and team workload.
- Backlogs – prioritized, flexible lists of requirements that continuously evolve based on stakeholder feedback and changing needs.

By focusing on interactions and tangible deliverables rather than extensive paperwork, Agile helps teams quickly adapt, deliver ongoing value and remain closely aligned with stakeholder expectations.

AGILE PROJECT STAGES

Agile doesn't use Waterfall stages but works in iterations or 'sprints'. A typical Agile process looks like the following outline. Please note that, unlike Waterfall, it doesn't flow sequentially:

1 Concept:
   - Taj Motor Group lacks a recruitment funnel that visualizes recruitment stages and conversion, making it difficult to determine hiring efficiency and identify bottlenecks.
   - Hold a focused kick-off meeting and confirm product ownership and stakeholder involvement (recruitment head, People Systems, department heads, HRBPs).

2 Backlog creation:

- Facilitate stakeholder workshops to collaboratively identify clear requirements, define user stories and estimate the effort required to deliver a minimum viable product (MVP)

- Capture requirements as user stories, e.g. 'As a recruitment head, I want to visualize candidate drop-off rates to identify recruitment bottlenecks', or 'As an HRBP, I want to filter hiring data by department to effectively monitor progress'.

- Co-create and prioritize the backlog with the product owner and key stakeholders, clearly identifying the essential dashboard features, functionalities and acceptance criteria necessary for the MVP.

- Document and track all tasks, user stories and related criteria using tools such as JIRA or Microsoft Planner.

3 Sprint/iteration planning:

- Book in sprint planning meetings at the start of each sprint, inviting stakeholders relevant to the tasks and features included in the sprint.

- Prioritize backlog tasks collaboratively, outlining activities, timelines and ownership on the Kanban or scrum board.

- Agree on immediate tasks to deliver value within the sprint.

4 Sprint execution:

- Drive the delivery of all agreed-upon tasks, including gathering recruitment data, agreeing on standardized definitions and iterative development of the dashboard in Power BI.

- Gather frequent feedback from stakeholders and use it to refine and enhance functionality incrementally to align with user needs and expectations.

5 Sprint review/demos:

- At the end of each sprint, hold review sessions or demos where the team presents completed dashboard functionalities to stakeholders, clearly demonstrating incremental progress.

6 Regular stand-ups and sprint retrospectives:

- Host regular daily stand-up meetings to ensure continuous alignment, identify blockers and maintain momentum.

- After each sprint, conduct short retrospectives capturing learnings, refining backlog priorities and improving delivery practice for the next sprint.

7 Backlog grooming:

- Regularly incorporate new insights and hold frequent 'stop, start, continue' discussions to adjust and reprioritize sprint tasks based on evolving stakeholder inputs and changing project requirements.

- Ensure the backlog remains accurate, clearly defined and closely aligned to stakeholder expectations.

- Update and refine user stories, clarify acceptance criteria, reprioritize tasks and remove outdated items to maintain a streamlined, actionable backlog that supports rapid and effective delivery.

TOP TIP
Find a course to learn more

As you can see, Agile project management is complex and includes a lot of principles and technical terminology that we can only touch on here. If you are interested in deepening your understanding of Agile, consider certifications such as:

- Certified ScrumMaster (CSM)

- Certified Scrum Product Owner (CSPO)

- Professional Scrum Master (PSM I & II)

- SAFe Agilist Certification (Scaled Agile Framework)
- PMI Agile Certified Practitioner (PMI-ACP)

The hybrid/balanced approach

Now that you have a good understanding of the Waterfall and Agile methodologies, let's turn to the hybrid approach, which we touched on earlier in this chapter. This approach is particularly prevalent in HR and shared services environments. It is a pragmatic way of transforming input into output, leveraging elements of Waterfall and Agile methodology as required. In such settings, you may encounter Agile concepts like iterations, features and MVPs alongside traditional elements such as detailed project plans, fixed budgets and strict timelines. This blend aims to leverage the strengths of both methodologies to address the unique challenges faced in HR projects.

Hybrid gives enough structure to keep deadlines realistic and progress measurable while allowing for flexibility when business needs change and offering a more customer-focused approach. You can also tailor the degree to which you apply Agile and Waterfall based on the project environment and stakeholders. If the project is time and budget-bound and stakeholders require certainty over creativity, you can utilize an approach that is more Waterfall-focused, and vice versa.

WHAT WOULD YOU DO?
Number 2

Earlier in this chapter, you were asked to consider whether you would apply a Waterfall, Agile or hybrid approach to the project at Taj Motor Group. Presuming you chose a hybrid approach, write a detailed plan of how you would put this into practice, choosing elements of Waterfall and Agile to produce a bespoke approach that will guarantee delivery by the offsite in six weeks.

STOP AND THINK

Think about a recent project you completed either at work or in your life. Would you approach it differently now that you learned about project management?

Common PA project management challenges

There are some common challenges you might encounter when managing projects as a PA professional:

- There is no project (until you create one) – PA is often asked for reports rather than projects, so sometimes you need to invent the project, find a sponsor and pitch the need for a project. This might involve spotting patterns in recurring ad hoc requests, connecting them to business outcomes and pitching them as a scalable initiative.
- Stakeholder turnover – when key sponsors leave mid-project, you lose context, time and access to decision-makers. New stakeholders may not share the original pain point or see the need for the project. Keep your stakeholder map 'live' and maintain a project pitching document including the goal, assumptions, context, timeline and early feedback.
- Internal politics – PA projects can sometimes threaten existing power structures, particularly automation projects. HRBPs, Talent Operations or Workforce Planning teams might feel like you are stepping on toes with your project, even if your goal is collaboration and the outcome is mutually beneficial. This can quietly stall access to data, slow feedback loops or block progress. Lean towards Agile and treat concerned stakeholders as co-owners, having frequent 'heart-to-hearts' with them. Communicate your acceptance of their fear and how you are working towards not allowing those fears to materialize.

- Paralysis from 'decision by committee' – projects can get delayed waiting for sign-off with stakeholders reluctant to make the final call on decisions. Part of clarifying stakeholders is identifying decision-makers up front. Set your expectations regularly by clarifying dates by which decisions need to be made. If nobody cares enough to own decisions, consider whether the project is worth doing.

CHAPTER SUMMARY

- Applying structured project management approaches to PA work allows you to manage multiple stakeholders, plan effectively while remaining flexible, communicate well, collaborate and deliver.

- Waterfall follows a rigid structure and relies on documentation to communicate progress. Agile is more flexible and delivers work in short, iterative sprints. Regular communication, ceremonies and tools are used instead of documentation. A hybrid approach combines elements of both and is often the most practical in real-world scenarios.

- When deciding on an approach, consider factors like context, project environment and stakeholder expectations. A hybrid approach is often best, and it can be tailored to rely more heavily on Waterfall or Agile depending on time, budget and stakeholder preferences.

- Projects can face many challenges, such as losing key sponsors or a lack of buy-in from key players in the organization. Do what you can to anticipate any potential pitfalls and mitigate the risk of them tripping you up.

REVIEW QUESTIONS

1 Why is it important for people analytics professionals to understand project management?

2   What are some documentations that a project manager will
    produce and how does it differ between Agile, Waterfall and
    hybrid project management?

3   List two benefits and two limitations for Agile project
    management and Waterfall project management.

Endnotes

1   Adobe (2023) Learn How to Use the Input-Process-Output (IPO)
    Model, Adobe Business Blog, https://business.adobe.com/blog/basics/
    learn-about-the-input-output-model (archived at https://perma.cc/
    WBF5-72Z7)

2   Yang, S and Lechler, T (2014) Project Management Process Models as
    Antecedents for Job Satisfaction: A Comparative Analysis of Waterfall
    and Scrum, PMI, 29 July, https://www.pmi.org/learning/library/
    project-management-process-models-job-satisfaction-1921 (archived
    at https://perma.cc/P72S-5YNC)

3   Burgan, S C and Burgan, D S (2014) One Size Does Not Fit All:
    Choosing the Right Project Approach, PMI, 26 October, www.pmi.
    org/learning/library/choosing-right-project-approach-9346 (archived
    at https://perma.cc/KAH6-V4K5)

4   Institute of Project Management (2022) What is the Waterfall
    Methodology?, Institute of Project Management, https://
    instituteprojectmanagement.com/blog/waterfall-methodology
    (archived at https://perma.cc/54W2-KUD7)

5   Sliger, M (2011) Agile Project Management with Scrum, PMI,
    22 October, www.pmi.org/learning/library/agile-project-management-
    scrum-6269 (archived at https://perma.cc/EB37-Z48S)

6   Project Management Institute (2024) Hybrid Project Management:
    Fit-for-Purpose to Drive Performance, Project Management,
    12 March, www.projectmanagement.com/webinars/937736/hybrid-
    project-management--fit-for-purpose-to-drive-performance- (archived
    at https://perma.cc/FUR9-67JT)

7   Project Management Institute (2021) 12 Principles of Project
    Management, PMI, www.pmi.org/-/media/pmi/documents/public/pdf/
    pmbok-standards/12-project-management-principles.pdf (archived at
    https://perma.cc/KAQ7-P3F9)

CHAPTER FIVE

Managing change through people analytics

Introduction

Now that we have explored what people analytics is, how to build strong relationships and manage projects effectively, it is time to connect that good work with a lasting impact.

If project management is the house's foundation, then change management is the plumbing. It keeps things flowing, connects all the parts, and ensures that what's been built works for the people living in it. Without it, even the best-designed solutions struggle to function as intended.

In this chapter, we deep dive into this powerful (and often overlooked) skill that can truly set you apart from other analytics professionals. Data and insights are only part of the story. Real value occurs when people act on those insights, when organizations adapt, and when change takes hold. That is what change management can help you with. We explore why change management is important, a six-step change management process and core change management principles, frameworks and tools, many of which operate beneath the surface but are vital for driving meaningful progress. Equipping yourself to apply these 'unspoken' techniques in your day-to-day work will enable you to manage change (and resistance) with empathy, clarity and strategic thinking.

LEARNING OBJECTIVES

By the end of this chapter, you will be able to:

- Appreciate why change management is fundamental to a successful career in people analytics.

- Develop a six-step process to manage your next change management project, no matter how large or small.

- Describe six change management methodologies and when to apply them.

- Explain what motivates people to change, and understand how to utilize intrinsic and extrinsic motivation to get the best results.

Why is change management important?

What is change? At its core, it is the act of shifting from one state to another. Change management is the process of guiding that movement. It is about helping people and organizations move through change thoughtfully, so the transition does not just happen; it sustains and benefits until the next transformation begins.

Learning about change management can benefit you enormously in people analytics, from running an organization-wide transformation to dealing with difficult stakeholders, building a people analytics function, or coaching a team member to deal with an upsetting piece of news. Influencing and inspiring others is part of the job, but you rarely hear how you can learn these skills. The answer is simple: change management.

People analytics as a function was born out of change and driven by a need to bring clarity and insight to people decisions, given the rise of systems and technology that unlocked new possibilities with data. With the rise of AI and autonomous agents, change is everywhere. Your role in each of these situations might vary – you could be leading the change, supporting it or simply affected by it. But no matter where you sit, developing change management skills can make all the difference. These skills can help you navigate the practical and emotional impact of change on yourself and equip you to support others as they transition through it.

The change management process

Just like project management, we can use a linear process to describe the act of change management. This makes it easier, so you can absorb and apply the knowledge. The six-step process that follows is inspired by insights and best practices from a range of established frameworks.

Step 1: Clarify and agree

Before anything changes, it is important to be clear about what we are trying to achieve and whether change is even the right move. It is easy to rush into action, but without proper clarity, you can end up solving the wrong problem or even creating new ones.

For larger-scale change, there should be a clear objective, a strong business case, and visible backing. That usually means having a dedicated sponsor to champion the change and, ideally, a steering committee to help shape decisions and keep things aligned. Without that kind of structure, the whole thing can lose focus or stall before it even gets going.

Smaller changes are usually more informal. You might just need one key stakeholder who is willing to think differently or try a new approach. But even then, it is worth pausing to reflect. What is the real reason behind the change? Is it the right thing to do, not just for you but for the wider team, organization and community?

It is about asking honest questions early on, before anyone has invested time, money or energy. If the foundations are not solid, no amount of implementation will fix it later.

Step 2: Planting the seed

After we have a clear understanding and agreement on the need for change, the next step is to prepare minds for what is coming. This is where priming comes in. Priming is a concept from cognitive psychology that describes how exposure to certain cues or stimuli can influence our later thoughts and actions without us even realizing it.[1]

Research has shown that priming can subtly shape our behaviour and attitudes by activating related ideas in our minds.[2] Essentially, when people are exposed to a particular stimulus, it can make them more receptive to related concepts later.

In the context of change management, priming helps ease the transition by making the change feel less abrupt and more natural. There are three steps:

1 **Start with pain point sessions**
   Bring people together (cross-functional and cross job ranks) into a safe and open space. Encourage everyone to share their frustrations about the current system or process. No filters, no hierarchy, just honest reflection. This process does two things: it gives people a voice, and it gives you language and insight you can use later. The pain points people share often become the benefits you can highlight when you introduce the new system.
2 **Equip leaders with relatable stories**
   Once you have a sense of what matters to people, curate a few real-world examples, either from other parts of the business or similar companies, to show how others have faced similar issues and what changed as a result. Pass these

on to line managers and community leaders so they can build them into their conversations.

3 **Repeat the pain points to reinforce the need**
Repeat pain points subtly but intentionally. Add them into team chats, updates and informal catch-ups to gently reinforce the shared sense that something needs to shift. That way, when change is officially on the table, people see it as a response to their concerns, not an external imposition.

Using these priming techniques, instead of dropping an idea on your team, you are gradually warming them up to a shift in thinking. When a formal announcement or detailed plan is presented, people have already started to see the change as a natural and logical next step.

Step 3: Lead by example

This is the point where things start to shift from ideas into action. It is time to set the direction and create momentum with clarity, intention and care.

At this stage, leadership backing becomes essential. Whether it is a formal sponsor or a key figure in the organization, their support needs to be visible and felt. But it's not about hierarchy or command. The most effective sponsors lead with passion, not pressure. They speak about the change with energy and belief, not just because they have been told to, but because they genuinely care about the outcome.

People don't get behind change because someone with a title tells them to. They get behind it when they see someone they respect believe in it. The role of leadership here is to inspire the change, not enforce it.[3] A well-timed statement from a people leader like 'I care about this and I believe in it' goes much further than ticking a box or issuing a directive.

We need to note that timing is critical here. If leaders show up too early, before people have been primed or understand the reasons, it can feel forced. But if the groundwork is laid, their support acts like fuel. It legitimizes the change and permits it to move forward.

This is also the time for leaders to provide structure. People need certainty, which can be delivered through governance in the form of clarifying who will be involved in the ongoing decisions, what the rhythm of communication is, and how progress will be reviewed. People also need reassurance, which can be done by clarifying what is not changing. This helps people feel grounded, not destabilized.

Smaller changes may not need formal leadership involvement; you may be the sponsor, so show up and lead the change with your own energy. The same rule applies, inspire with purpose instead of pressure. If you don't believe in it, no one else will.

TOP TIP
Find the right balance

Leading change is all about balance. Stay firm on what needs to happen and when, but remain fair and hold space for people's reactions. Feedback, pushback, uncertainty, all of that still has room. Remember the definition of leadership – inspire people to move, don't command them to follow.

Step 4: Incremental shifts and nudging

Trying to change everything at once never works for sustainable change. It overwhelms people, creates pushback and often leads to half-finished ideas. Instead, focus on small, well-timed shifts such as subtle nudges that build progress step by step.

Behavioural design expert Nir Eyal believes that we don't need to force people into action, we just need to make the desired behaviour the easiest, most natural choice in the moment. By reducing friction, offering simple next steps and framing actions in a way that feels intuitive, he suggests that we can gently guide people towards change without overwhelming them.[4]

In practice, this looks like:

- Starting with low-risk pilots where people can safely explore the new way of working.
- Offering tools, templates or walkthroughs that make the new behaviour easier than sticking with the old one.
- Highlighting quick wins to build confidence and create a sense of progress.
- Using regular check-ins and nudges (not demands) to remind and encourage without applying pressure.

Step 5: Overeducate

When people are confused, repeat the message differently. Then repeat it again, sharing it across various platforms.

In modern workplaces, we often work across different time zones, cultures, communication styles and access needs. Some people are in the room, some are dialling in from home, some are catching up two days later, and everyone processes information differently. Ensure no one misses out because of where they sit, how they work or their different learning styles.

> **TOP TIP**
> Don't rely on one version of the message
>
> Send a write-up, record a quick video, drop a note in the chat and follow up in the next team meeting. Make time for questions, even if they feel basic. If one person asks, a few others are probably wondering the same thing.

Step 6: Relapse prevention

Even when change is technically complete, the work is not over. It is easy to assume the job is done once the dashboard is live or the new process is rolled out, but that is usually when the real work begins.

Old habits have a funny way of creeping back in, especially when people get busy and stressed. Dashboards can get lots of attention in the first week and barely be touched after that, as people quietly return to spreadsheets. It is not because people are against the change; it is usually because it is familiar, quicker in the moment, or they did not fully understand how the new way helped them. Slipping back is not a failure, it is feedback.

TOP TIP
Keep nudging[5]

Don't stop nudging once the change is live. Keep a close eye on how people are working. If they have returned to the old way, ask *why?*

- Was the new process clunky?
- Did it make life harder?
- Did the benefits get lost in the day-to-day pressure?

The answers will provide valuable feedback to help you improve the approach.

Sometimes, you may reach a point where you must cut off Plan B, so people fully commit to Plan A. Maybe that means disabling access to the old system, removing an outdated template, or switching off an unofficial workaround. Make these moves carefully and intentionally. Forcing people to commit without the right support or timing can backfire badly. Treat removing the backup option as a change, and follow the six-step process.

The change adoption curve

Your next question might be, 'You have shared the process for change management, but when do we go from one stage to another?' This is when the understanding of the Kubler-Ross change curve sets in. The Kubler-Ross Change Curve was originally developed to describe how people process grief, but it has been widely adapted to explain how we move through emotional responses to change.[6] While timing varies by person, most follow a predictable emotional journey. You can align your actions to this curve:

- Step 1 (Clarify and Agree) – people are in the pre-shock phase, they are calm, sceptical or curious, you should spend time to build on shared understanding.
- Step 2 (Planting the Seed) – shock and denial may set in, you can now prepare people through storytelling and conversation.
- Step 3 (Firm by Fair) – resistance peaks while people feel frustration and anger, this is when you should set expectations, lead with empathy and listen actively.
- Step 4 (Incremental Shifts and Nudging) – people start experimenting, this is when you want to support small wins and low-risk trials.
- Step 5 (Overeducate) – acceptance grows, this is the time to reinforce learning through frequent, varied communication.
- Step 6 (Relapse Prevention) – this is the time for integration, habits start to form but they may slip, this is when you should keep nudging, watch for regression and remove fallback options while building readiness.

Change management toolbox

The kinds of problems change management can help solve range from everyday challenges to large-scale transformations. Just like a skilled tradie, it is important to be familiar with the full set of tools available. Because if you only have a hammer, every problem can look like a nail.

This section introduces several change management tools and methodologies so you can start building a sense of which tools to use and when to use them.

Change management methodologies

A lot of change management methodologies exist, and they can be confusing. The reality is that things are not that absolute; change professionals often combine techniques based on the different environmental variables they encounter, which is very similar to the hybrid/balanced approach to project management we learned about in Chapter 4. Some of these are change management purist models, which means they are invented for the sake of change management, while others can be applied widely to many other scenarios.

Throughout this section, use the Tamari Bank real-world example and 'What would you do?' questions to reflect on the relationship between the six change models and their applicability to different problems. The answers to the 'What would you do?' questions can be found in the Appendix.

REAL-WORLD EXAMPLE
Data literacy project at Tamari Bank

Tamari is a large financial institution with a deeply rooted HR function, with over 1,000 professionals managing everything from talent acquisition to offboarding. The organization is undergoing a major digital transformation: the executive board has set a clear mandate to digitize HR to make it ready for the emergence of AI-driven operations.

However, a recent internal survey has surfaced a critical challenge. Over 80 per cent of HR professionals self-report an elementary level of data literacy. Many express a sense of discomfort and intimidation when it comes to working with digital systems, formulas or data analytics tools. There is widespread hesitation, both technical and emotional. For many, data represents complexity, unfamiliar territory and a threat to their established roles.

Your task is to raise the level of data literacy across the HR team.

ADKAR MODEL (PROSCI)

ADKAR is a goal-oriented model for individual change, created by Jeff Hiatt, founder of the Prosci organization. Unlike many frameworks that focus on organizational structures or strategy, ADKAR operates from the premise that successful change happens one person at a time. It breaks the change process into five outcomes that must occur in sequence:[7]

1 Awareness of the need for change.
2 Desire to support and participate in the change.
3 Knowledge of how to change.
4 Ability to implement new behaviours or skills.
5 Reinforcement to sustain the change over time.

The model is built on the psychology of motivation and learning, acknowledging that resistance is natural and often emotional. ADKAR's power lies in its diagnostic capability; it can help you identify where individuals are getting stuck.

- *Use it when*: You are addressing personal resistance, fear or low confidence (e.g. staff anxious about data).
- *Don't use it when*: You're shifting systems, organization design or strategy.
- *Why?* ADKAR is not designed for structural alignment. It focuses on behaviour and mindset.
- *Suitability for daily/informal coaching*: High – excellent for one-to-one coaching, informal mentoring and team support.

WHAT WOULD YOU DO?
Number 3

How would you apply this at Tamari Bank? ADKAR is essential to support the emotional side of your transformation. It is ideal for addressing individual resistance, especially the emotional and psychological discomfort many staff feel around data. Write a plan for how you would apply this model.

KOTTER'S 8-STEP CHANGE MODEL

Developed by Harvard Business School professor John P. Kotter in the mid-1990s, the 8-Step Change Model is one of the most widely used frameworks for leading organizational change. It outlines a top-down approach to initiating, implementing and sustaining transformational change within larger organizations.

The model assumes that successful change is not just about processes and systems but also about emotion and momentum. People change when they feel the urgency, brought into a compelling vision and guided by visible leadership. The eight steps are as follows:[8]

1 Create a sense of urgency.
2 Build a guiding coalition.
3 Form a strategic vision and initiatives.
4 Communicate the vision.
5 Remove obstacles.
6 Create short-term wins.
7 Sustain acceleration.
8 Anchor the changes in culture.

This model is particularly well-suited to large, hierarchical organizations where formal leadership plays a major role in shaping norms and where long-standing cultural practices may slow innovation.[9]

- *Use it when*: You need to lead visible, organization-wide transformation with leadership involvement.
- *Don't use it when*: You're running small pilots, need fast iteration or lack senior buy-in.
- *Why?* Kotter assumes formal authority and long timeframes. It is too heavyweight for informal use.
- *Suitability for daily/informal coaching*: Low – best suited for formal initiatives. It's not practical for daily interactions.

> **WHAT WOULD YOU DO?**
> Number 4
>
> How would you use Kotter's model to structure a bank-wide movement towards a culture of data literacy?

LEWIN'S THREE PHASES OF CHANGE

Kurt Lewin, a German-American psychologist and pioneer of social psychology, proposed a foundational model for managing change in the 1940s. His framework, though simple, remains influential because it captures the emotional dynamics of behaviour change.

The model breaks change into three sequential phases:

1 Unfreeze – people are helped to let go of current beliefs, behaviours or routines.
2 Change – new behaviours or processes are introduced and tested.
3 Refreeze – new habits are reinforced until they become the new normal.

Lewin believed that people resist change not because they are irrational, but because their behaviours are 'frozen' in a social and organizational context. Change, therefore, must first disrupt the equilibrium and later stabilize it again.[10]

This model is ideal for emotionally charged or identity-related change at a group or individual level, such as shifting a professional mindset away from 'following the process' to 'problem-solving'.

- *Use it when*: You are managing emotionally sensitive or identity-based change.
- *Don't use it when*: The change is continuous or evolving without a clear end state.

- *Why?* Lewin assumes a discrete beginning, middle and end. It's therefore less useful in Agile.
- *Suitability for daily/informal coaching*: Medium – useful in coaching to validate feelings and help someone 'unfreeze'. It's less suited to rapid or iterative contexts.

WHAT WOULD YOU DO?
Number 5

How can you use Lewin's model and its related concepts to help manage the emotional and psychological transition of people during the change?

MCKINSEY'S 7S MODEL

Developed by McKinsey & Company in the late 1970s, the 7S Framework is designed to help organizations assess and align the key components that drive performance and change. The seven elements are:[11]

1 Strategy – the organization's plan for competing and winning.
2 Structure – how roles and responsibilities are organized.
3 Systems – processes, procedures and technology.
4 Shared values – organizational culture and guiding principles.
5 Style – leadership behaviour and communication.
6 Staff – capabilities and people.
7 Skills – the actual competencies within the organization.

The model emphasizes interconnectedness of the organizational system, you cannot change one element (e.g. skills) without affecting the others. It is a systems-level tool to ensure alignment and coherence across multiple aspects of an organization. This model is suitable for organizational/large-scale change and ensures that as many aspects of the organization are considered and incorporated into the change plan as possible.

- *Use it when*: You need to assess alignment across systems, skills and values.
- *Don't use it when*: You are focused on individual skill or team-level behaviour.
- *Why?* It's too abstract and strategic for individual coaching.
- *Suitability for daily/informal coaching*: Low – it's primarily a diagnostic tool for formal transformation and is rarely used in day-to-day coaching.

WHAT WOULD YOU DO?
Number 6

Where might the 7S model be applicable in Tamari Bank's case? How would you apply it?

GROW MODEL

The GROW model is not an official change management framework, but it is an invaluable tool for supporting change. Originally developed in the 1980s as a coaching framework, GROW helps individuals and teams move from uncertainty to clarity through structured reflection, goal setting and action planning. It provides a simple, human-centred roadmap for progress. GROW stands for:[12]

- Goal – define a clear and motivating objective.
- Reality – explore the current state, including barriers and concerns.
- Options – identify strategies, ideas and resources to move forward.
- Way forward – commit to specific actions and next steps.

Unlike traditional change frameworks, GROW is conversational, adaptable and easy to apply. It is particularly helpful when teams are navigating both technical change and emotional uncertainty. It complements technical change by supporting emotional and cognitive shifts. It can give you structure to the messiness of learning and help people own their progress.

- *Use it when*: You want to support individuals or teams through change by building clarity, confidence and commitment.
- *Don't use it when*: You're setting vision or dealing with deep-rooted emotional resistance.
- *Why?* GROW is conversational, not strategic. It's less effective for complex, system-wide change without broader alignment.
- *Suitability for daily/informal coaching*: High – great for coaching sessions, development planning and change conversations at a team or individual level.

WHAT WOULD YOU DO?
Number 7

How would you use GROW model to guide HR team members' transition towards data literacy?

LEAN THINKING AND CONTINUOUS IMPROVEMENT

Lean originated in post-World War II Japan, particularly through Toyota's production system, and was later adapted for broader organizational use. It emphasizes the elimination of non-value adding waste while focusing on end user value, continuous improvement and using small-scale pilots and iterative feedback.[13]

At its core is the PDCA cycle (Plan, Do, Check, Act),[14] which encourages teams to test ideas, measure their effectiveness and refine based on evidence. Lean is especially useful in environments where agility, adaptability and frontline insight are needed to improve performance sustainably.

- *Use it when*: You want to test, learn and improve quickly through feedback.

- *Don't use it when*: You're setting vision or dealing with deep-rooted emotional resistance
- *Why?* Lean is operational, not emotional. It needs systems or data to work from.
- *Suitability for daily/informal coaching*: High – great for daily retrospectives, process coaching and informal improvement conversations.

WHAT WOULD YOU DO?
Number 8

Where can you apply lean thinking and continuous improvement methods in Tamari Bank on the data literacy project?

Motivation

Often, learning about the frameworks is not enough; understanding what truly motivates people is another key aspect of change management. Those managing change need to realize that people have unique reasons for their reactions to it; it's important not to make assumptions and manage emotions as they arise. Research from Deci and Ryan's Self-Determination Theory[15] shows that people are more likely to engage and perform well when they feel autonomous, competent and connected. If you can understand what drives someone, you will be able to meet them where they are and help them feel that change is a necessary part of the journey to get to where their goals are. Change then becomes something they choose to be involved in, not just something that happens to them.

Motivation can come from all kinds of places, according to Ryan and Deci's research, there are two major categories.[16] Intrinsic motivation is associated with passion, interest and fulfilment. It can come from a sense of ownership, purpose and curiosity. Extrinsic motivation, on the other hand, is associated more with external rewards like pay, recognition or avoiding consequences.

INTRINSIC MOTIVATION

People respond to change most effectively when their intrinsic motivation is recognized and supported first. For example, if a team member feels the change will help them grow, take on more meaningful work or solve a challenge they care about, they are much more likely to engage with genuine energy.

TOP TIP
Appeal to people's intrinsic motivation

Try to frame transitions as an opportunity to learn something new, make a meaningful contribution, or take more control. Giving people space to voice ideas, ask questions and shape the outcome themselves activates their inner drive.

EXTRINSIC MOTIVATION

While recognition, rewards, promotions and other monetary benefits can be useful, especially when they acknowledge real effort or progress, try not to use this as the main driver to get someone to act. Research has discovered the over-justification effect, which shows that when people are overly motivated by external rewards, it can decrease their natural interest in the task.[17] This is because the external rewards can make people feel like they are only taking actions because of the reward, not because they believe in the change or find value in the work.

TOP TIP
Use extrinsic motivators wisely

Use extrinsic motivators sparingly and intentionally to reinforce momentum, not replace meaning.

The sweet spot is when intrinsic motivation does the heavy lifting, and external rewards act as the cherry on top. Intrinsic motivation tends to be more sustainable over time, while extrinsic motivation can be powerful in the short term. They can be utilized differently throughout change and influence initiatives, if you need to reward someone's temporary change of behaviour. Motivation can also be internalized, where external goals are adopted because they align with someone's personal values. Understanding these different layers will help you support people in ways that work for them.

CHAPTER SUMMARY

- Change management skills are vital for people analytics professionals, from persuading someone sceptical of our insights to helping teams accept digital tools that may alter their roles. Your ability to manage resistance to change will define your influence throughout your career.

- Change is most effective when a linear process is followed to clarify and agree on the need for change before gradually introducing the change and nudging people towards it.

- People's reaction to change often follows a predictable pattern as outlined by the change adoption curve, which you can use to help manage the change.

- Several change management methodologies exist, some of which were invented for change management, while others can be used in many other scenarios. It is often most effective to use a hybrid approach, picking elements of different methodologies to suit the problem and specific circumstances.

- Understanding what motivates people can help you communicate and execute change. It's important to understand the difference between intrinsic and extrinsic motivation and when to acknowledge and support each type.

REVIEW QUESTIONS

1   What difference will it make if you manage the change properly versus if you don't manage change? Think about a recent project that you had to deliver to answer this question.

2   What are the main change management methodologies covered in this chapter and how will you use them to help improve data literacy within your PA role?

3   Think about a recent scenario where you had to do something you didn't want to do. Which type of motivation drove you? Is it intrinsic or extrinsic motivation? Or a combination of both?

Endnotes

1   Horner, A J and Henson, R N (2008) Priming, Response Learning, and Repetition Suppression, *Neuropsychologia*, 46(7), 1979–91, https://www.sciencedirect.com/science/article/pii/S0028393208000535 (archived at https://perma.cc/2BYN-FAPJ)

2   Bargh, J A, Chen, M and Burrows, L (1996) Automaticity of Social Behavior: Direct Effects of Trait Construct and Stereotype Activation on Action, *Journal of Personality and Social Psychology*, 71(2), 230–44, https://doi.org/10.1037/0022-3514.71.2.230 (archived at https://perma.cc/3T4Q-7S5K)

3   Oxford Global Resources (2022) The Importance of Executive Sponsors and Change Champions in Organizational Change Management, Oxford Global Resources, https://www.oxfordcorp.com/insights/blog/the-importance-of-change-agents-sponsors-and-champions-in-organizational-change-management/ (archived at https://perma.cc/V9V7-JV4E)

4   Eyal, N (2014) *Hooked: How to Build Habit-Forming Products*, Penguin

5   Thaler, R H and Sunstein, C R (2009) *Nudge: Improving Decisions About Health*, Wealth and Happiness, Penguin Books

6   Kübler-Ross, E and Kessler, D (2009) *On Grief and Grieving*, Scribner

7   Prosci Inc (2024) The Prosci ADKAR Model Overview, Prosci, www.prosci.com/ADKAR (archived at https://perma.cc/QW5E-FVBR)

8   Kotter, J P (1996) *Leading Change*, Harvard Business School Press

9   Davis, J (2022) Dewey Goes Corporate: Examining the Suitability of
    Kotter's Change Management Model for Use in Libraries, *Journal of
    Library Administration*, 62, 275–90, https://www.tandfonline.com/
    doi/full/10.1080/01930826.2022.2043687 (archived at https://
    perma.cc/WUZ3-NLUH)
10 Lewin, K (1947) Frontiers in Group Dynamics: Concept, Method
    and Reality in Social Science; Social Equilibria and Social Change,
    Human Relations, 1(1), 5–41 https://journals.sagepub.com/doi/
    10.1177/001872674700100103 (archived at https://perma.cc/
    Q83E-FD7Q)
11 Waterman, R H, Peters, T J and Phillips, J R (1980) Structure Is Not
    Organization, *Business Horizons*, 23(3), 14–26, https://www.
    sciencedirect.com/science/article/abs/pii/0007681380900270
    (archived at https://perma.cc/4NQG-HZGV)
12 Whitmore, J (2009) *Coaching for Performance: Growing Human
    Potential and Purpose – The Principles and Practice of Coaching and
    Leadership*, 4th edn, Nicholas Brealey Publishing
13 Yamamoto, K, Milstead, M and Lloyd, R A (2019) A Review of the
    Development of Lean Manufacturing and Related Lean Practices:
    The Case of Toyota Production System and Managerial Thinking,
    International Management Review, 15(2), 21–90, https://www.
    researchgate.net/publication/340449306 (archived at https://perma.cc/
    YJF6-K24P)
14 Nguyen, V, Chau, C K B and Tran, T (2023) PDCA from Theory to
    Effective Applications: A Case Study of Design for Reducing Human
    Error in Assembly Process, *Advances in Operations Research*, Article
    ID 8007474, 9, https://onlinelibrary.wiley.com/doi/10.1155/2023/
    8007474 (archived at https://perma.cc/C3CR-AK54)
15 Deci, E L and Ryan, R M (1985) Intrinsic Motivation and Self-
    Determination in Human Behavior, Plenum Press, https://link.
    springer.com/book/10.1007/978-1-4899-2271-7 (archived at
    https://perma.cc/7CFA-49YB)
16 Ryan, R M and Deci, E L (2000) Intrinsic and Extrinsic Motivations:
    Classic Definitions and New Directions, *Contemporary Educational
    Psychology*, 25(1), 54–67, https://www.sciencedirect.com/science/article/
    pii/S0361476X99910202 (archived at https://perma.cc/75AW-FBAC)
17 Deci, E L (1971) Effects of Externally Mediated Rewards on Intrinsic
    Motivation, *Journal of Personality and Social Psychology*, 18(1),
    105–15, https://psycnet.apa.org/record/1971-22190-001 (archived at
    https://perma.cc/223Q-HXAD)

CHAPTER SIX

Consulting frameworks for people analytics

Introduction

This is the first of our more skills-based chapters, where you will start building your analytics toolkit. Each tool will be introduced gradually through a real-world example that unfolds over the next two chapters. As the story develops, you will learn when and how to use each method in a way that feels natural and grounded.

You do not need to grasp every technical detail right away. That's not the aim. Full understanding comes with experience. What matters now is getting a feel for what each tool can do, so later, when a similar challenge appears, you will recognize it and know where to look.

These tools are applicable across nearly all people analytics work. We zoom out at times to view them through a systems-thinking lens, connecting individual problems to the wider organization.

Ready? We start by introducing the real-world example. This chapter focuses on consulting frameworks, as these skills are necessary to use before diving into analysing a problem. Chapter

7 focuses on data frameworks, which you can use once you've clarified the problem, understood the business need and know how to guide stakeholders through it.

LEARNING OBJECTIVES

By the end of this chapter, you will be able to:

- Lead a discovery conversation to build trust with stakeholders and clarify the wider problem.
- Define assumptions to unpack problems and gain alignment.
- Use the MECE principle to break a problem down into distinct categories to use for your analysis.
- Outline an issue tree to shape hypotheses and structure your testing.
- Set the scope for your PA work and agree it with stakeholders.
- Conduct a simple process map to gain business acumen.

REAL-WORLD EXAMPLE
Leadership pipeline at a Japanese car manufacturer

You recently joined the PA team at a globally respected Japanese car manufacturer, known for precision and long-term thinking. Expectations are high, and your role is to support smarter, future-focused people decisions. You work with five other analysts, each covering a different HR area. Your focus is Organizational Development and Learning and Development, including analytics on leadership, succession and training.

The company began a major HR systems overhaul five years ago, rolling out a well-known HRIS one module at a time. The learning management system (LMS) is now live, improving access to training data. Performance management is still mid-transition, with data migration underway. This shift has caused disruption, and many teams are frustrated. In production, performance data sat in an unsupported legacy system, Miracule. In sales, reviews were tracked in inconsistent spreadsheets. Despite the friction, the new system is vital for unifying data and strengthening analysis.

Your first few weeks have focused on learning and connection. You've been meeting stakeholders, reviewing dashboards and mapping how data flows through the organization. Most of the work has been standard reporting and ad-hoc requests.

Then a meeting titled 'Leadership pipeline health' lands in your calendar. It's set up by Sakshi, the Organizational Development (OD) Director and includes Meredith, the Chief People Officer (CPO). You haven't worked directly with them yet, though you recall Sakshi mentioning that several senior leaders are expected to retire in the next five to seven years.

This will be your first strategic project. You need to explore the data, engage stakeholders and deliver clear, evidence-based insights.

Relevant consulting frameworks (pre-analysis)

Requests like the one in the real-world example can come in all shapes and sizes, and problems can be thrown at you in different formats. It might be a vague concern raised in a meeting, a request from a senior stakeholder, or simply someone asking, 'Can you check if we have a problem here?'

In small organizations, the ask often comes informally, maybe in a chat message or a quick call. The data infrastructure might be limited or scattered, and you are likely to have to create things from scratch. In medium- and large-sized organizations, requests are usually more structured. Sometimes you will work with specialized people analytics tools, but some requests will still require you to navigate legacy systems, data gaps and cross-functional inputs.

No matter the context, your role often starts well before any data is analysed. Your first task is to clarify the problem, understand the business need driving it and guide stakeholders through the thinking process. This is where consulting skills are essential. Being effective in people analytics is not just about working with data. It is about listening closely, asking the right questions, framing the issue clearly, and helping stakeholders narrow their focus to a clear set of options they can agree on.

When a meeting titled 'Leadership Pipeline Health' lands in your calendar, it sounds big and strategic. But instead of jumping straight into assumptions or planning analysis steps, this is your opportunity to pause.

Discovery conversation

This upcoming meeting is your first real tool for consulting: using a discovery conversation to shift from reactive to proactive.

A discovery conversation gives you and your stakeholders space to unpack the issue together before diving into data. It's where open dialogue happens, the scope is clarified and trust starts to build. You are not there to have all the answers, you are there to listen, ask good questions and figure out what's going on. What's behind the ask? What's the bigger picture? Getting clarity early keeps expectations realistic and helps you focus where it matters.

In this case, the door's already open. The meeting is booked, so you have a natural way in. But it won't always land in your calendar so neatly. Sometimes, the first request shows up as a quick message: 'Can you pull some data on training attendance?' Sounds simple, but often, there's more going on under the surface. That's your cue to pause and create space for a proper chat to better understand the context and what's driving the question.

When you are early in your PA career, offering this kind of structure might feel a bit bold. But it doesn't need to be too formal. You are not pitching anything; you are just offering to slow things down and make sense of the request together. Most people appreciate it. It gives them a moment to think and shows you are interested in solving the right problem, not just the one that's easiest to see.

Framing it as a shared conversation also takes the pressure off. You are not trying to be the expert who knows everything. You are just showing up with curiosity and building the kind of trust that great analysis depends on.

LISTENING

As an early career professional, sitting in a room with senior leaders can feel daunting. You might feel pressure to contribute quickly or offer smart solutions. But your greatest asset in this moment is your ability to listen.

Good discovery work begins with listening to the meaning behind the words. It's how you build trust, uncover what matters and lay the groundwork for meaningful analysis.

In this section, we explore practical ways to listen well: how to open the discussion, manage your inner voice and create space for others to think clearly.

OPEN WITH THE RIGHT QUESTION

A discovery conversation starts with how you open it. The first question you ask sets the tone and shows your intent. Are you here to tick a box, or are you genuinely curious about what your stakeholders are dealing with?

Knowing the difference between open and closed questions matters here.

Closed questions usually start with *Is*, *Do* or *Can*. They lead to quick yes or no answers.

An example is 'Do we already track this data?' These questions are handy for checking facts, but not great for digging deeper.[1]

Open questions start with *What* or *How* and invite people to think and explain. Getting comfortable with them is one of the core skills in discovery conversations. An example is 'Before we dive in, I'd love to understand what prompted this conversation. Can you help me understand a bit more?'. Even though you are talking, this is part of listening. You are creating space for the real issue to surface.

Sometimes, the stakeholder jumps in first, gives you all the context and ends with, 'Can you do this?'. This is especially common with individuals who have a 'driver' communication style (see Chapter 3) and like direct, action-focused requests. The challenge is, it corners you into a yes/no before you even understand the full ask. In these moments, open up the conversation and demonstrate your approach as a partner, not just a task-ticker. Say something like, 'If you don't mind, let's take this a step back…' or 'Please help me understand…'

By taking this approach, you can uncover what's really going on and build trust as you go. When people feel heard, they open up. And when they open up, the real work can begin.

TUNE INTO DIFFERENT LAYERS OF LISTENING

Once the conversation starts, your job is to listen to what sits underneath the words. In this case, you learn that the concern came up in a senior leadership meeting. Someone in the executive team noticed many executives in production and sales joined around the same time, which means a large number are nearing mandatory retirement. There is growing concern that the company does not have enough people ready to step into those roles. A renowned sound and communication expert, Julian Treasure shared with us three types of listening approaches:[2]

- **Outer listening:** What's being said? Notice key phrases and tone. Are they focused on the future, sounding confident, or unsure? Write down specific words like 'retirement wave' or 'not enough ready people' alongside emotional cues like urgency or concern.

- **Inner listening:** What's going on in your mind? It is easy to get distracted by planning your response or overthinking the next step. When that happens, bring your focus back. Use reflections like, 'So this came up when the leadership team looked at the retirement profile?' to stay present. Also, be aware of filters. Are you leaning into what feels familiar and ignoring what does not?
- **Created listening:** What kind of space are you creating? Are people opening up more as they speak? Use open body language, steady eye contact and a calm tone to show you are fully present. Pause before responding. Let silence do some of the work. It shows you are taking in what was said.

You might leave the meeting without a clear ask, but with a sharper view of the real concern. Here, it is not just about how many people are ready. It is whether the organization trusts its internal pipeline to manage a major leadership shift.

WHAT WOULD YOU DO?
Number 9

Back to the real-world example – as the meeting unfolds, the tone changes. What began as a discussion starts to feel tense. The Chief People Officer says, 'Why did we not know this earlier?' The OD Director replies, 'This only came up because of a comment. We are focused on the current leadership programme. We cannot do everything.'

In moments like this, staying quiet might feel safer, especially if you are early in your career. But this is where listening becomes steadying. Tension often comes from misalignment. What could you say to ease the tension, gain trust and bring clarity to the problem?

TOP TIP
How to distinguish signal from noise

Not every concern needs a full investigation. Some are valid early signals, while others are background noise that will fade. Follow these three steps to determine what's worth exploring:

1   **Has it come up more than three times?**
    If you've heard the same issue repeatedly, from different people or at different times, it's likely to be a real signal rather than one-off noise.

2   **Who raised it?**
    A concern from a senior decision-maker or someone close to the issue carries more weight than a general comment from someone less involved.

3   **How does it rank among your priorities?**
    Rank it against other tasks on your list, and check with your leader or sponsor before shifting your focus.

Follow these steps to focus on what matters and maximize your energy.

Outline assumptions

Based on what you are hearing, the concern is that the leadership pipeline might not be strong enough. But before diving into analysis, it's worth pausing to ask what assumptions this question is built on.

In PA, it is very easy to treat a request like the problem is already proven. But often, what sounds certain is a mix of assumptions no one has fully unpacked. If you skip that step, you risk solving the wrong problem or doing work that eventually becomes redundant.

This is where your role shifts to help clarify. What would need to be true for this risk to exist? Until assumptions are visible, the problem has not been defined.

WHAT WOULD YOU DO?
Number 10

How would you define the assumptions in this case? List the assumptions that seem to be driving the concern so that you know what to base your analysis on, and outline how you would get stakeholders to agree.

TOP TIP
Foot-in-the-door technique

Get stakeholders to agree with you early, especially on small, low-risk points. It can make them more open to collaborating with you later. This is a principle from social psychology known as the 'foot-in-the-door' technique. If someone agrees to a small request, they are more likely to agree to a larger one later, as people like to stay consistent with their previous actions.[3]

Getting stakeholders to confirm the assumptions behind their concern helps to build alignment and commitment. Everyone agrees on what you should work on, which is more likely to make them stay engaged as you move into analysis and recommendations.

It's all about creating a shared foundation that makes collaboration smoother and more effective.

Mutually exclusive, collectively exhaustive

Once you have clarified assumptions, your next move is to organize the problem in a way that's structured and manageable. One of the simplest but most powerful tools for this is the MECE principle. It's the first of three principles discussed in this chapter and Chapter 7 that was invented by Barbara Minto at McKinsey.[4]

MECE stands for mutually exclusive, collectively exhausting. Mutually exclusive means each part of your analysis should be distinct. No overlaps, no duplication. Collectively exhaustive means your parts, taken together, should cover as much of the problem as possible with minimal gaps left behind.[5]

In PA, where challenges are frequently posed to you ambiguously, MECE helps you break a big, messy concern into clean lines of inquiry.

COMMON MECE CATEGORIES

The good news is, you don't have to come up with categories from scratch every time. There's a kind of mental library of common MECE categories that analysts and consultants often use. These include:

- Internal versus external.
- Supply versus demand.
- Short-term versus long-term.
- Leading versus lagging.
- Quantitative versus qualitative.
- Top-down versus bottom-up.
- Strategic versus operational.
- Monetary versus non-monetary.
- Cost versus benefit.
- Pros versus cons.
- Tangible versus intangible.
- Direct versus indirect.
- Collective versus individualized.

These are useful starting points when framing any problem. Start with memorizing them, and over time, you will find yourself reaching for them naturally, like using tools from a well-organized kit.

WHAT WOULD YOU DO?
Number 11

How would you apply the MECE principle to the problem: What is the risk that our leadership pipeline won't be strong enough to meet future needs? Which lens or lenses could you use from the categories above to structure the problem-solving process?

Issue tree

Once you've broken down a strategic problem into MECE categories, the next step is to go one level deeper. This is where the issue tree comes in.

An issue tree helps you map out the specific questions that sit underneath a broader challenge. It's like a branching set of mini problems, each of which can be explored and answered with data or input. This structure brings clarity to your thinking, helps you explain your process to stakeholders and prioritize what to analyse first.[6]

This is exactly what consultants do in the early phase of problem-solving. Before any data is pulled, they build an issue tree to shape their hypothesis and plan the work. It acts like a thinking blueprint showing where to focus, what to test and how to structure interviews, research or analysis. Consultants often walk clients through the tree to check alignment: 'Do these loos like the right drivers of the problem?' or 'Would you agree that these are the areas we need to explore first?'

It's a tool for thinking, and it keeps everyone anchored to the bigger picture. In PA, using an issue tree shows that you are not just chasing numbers; you are leading a structured investigation. It helps you avoid tunnel vision, manage expectations and build trust early in the project.

Let's apply the issue tree to our real-world example, and look at how demand and supply can be divided into branches (Figure 6.1).

FIRST BRANCH: DEMAND FOR LEADERSHIP

This branch helps you understand the leadership roles that will be needed soon. It can be divided into two sub-branches, with each one having several further sub-branches.

- Sub-branch 1: How many roles are likely to become vacant?
  - Are any leaders planning to retire or move on?
  - Are there known changes ahead (e.g. job changes, restructuring)?

- Sub-branch 2: Where are these roles mostly found?
  - Which departments or teams will be most affected?
  - Are there specific regions or levels where the risk is higher?
  - How important are these roles according to the skills and knowledge they possess?

SECOND BRANCH: SUPPLY OF LEADERSHIP-READY TALENT

This branch of the tree looks at how well the organization is positioned to meet that demand and where gaps might appear. It can be divided into three sub-branches with several sub-branches each.

- Sub-branch 1: Recruitment
  - Are we hiring people who could grow into leadership roles?
  - Are external hires progressing into leadership fast enough?
- Sub-branch 2: Turnover
  - Are potential future leaders staying with the company?
  - Are there areas where key people are leaving more often?
- Sub-branch 3: Promotion
  - Are high-potential people moving up as expected?
  - Is anything slowing down their progress?

These questions give you a full view of where the pipeline might break down and where it is holding strong.

WHAT WOULD YOU DO?
Number 12

How would you pitch these MECE categories and the issue tree to Sakshi and Meredith to make the problem feel structured and solvable?

FIGURE 6.1 Illustration of the Issue Tree

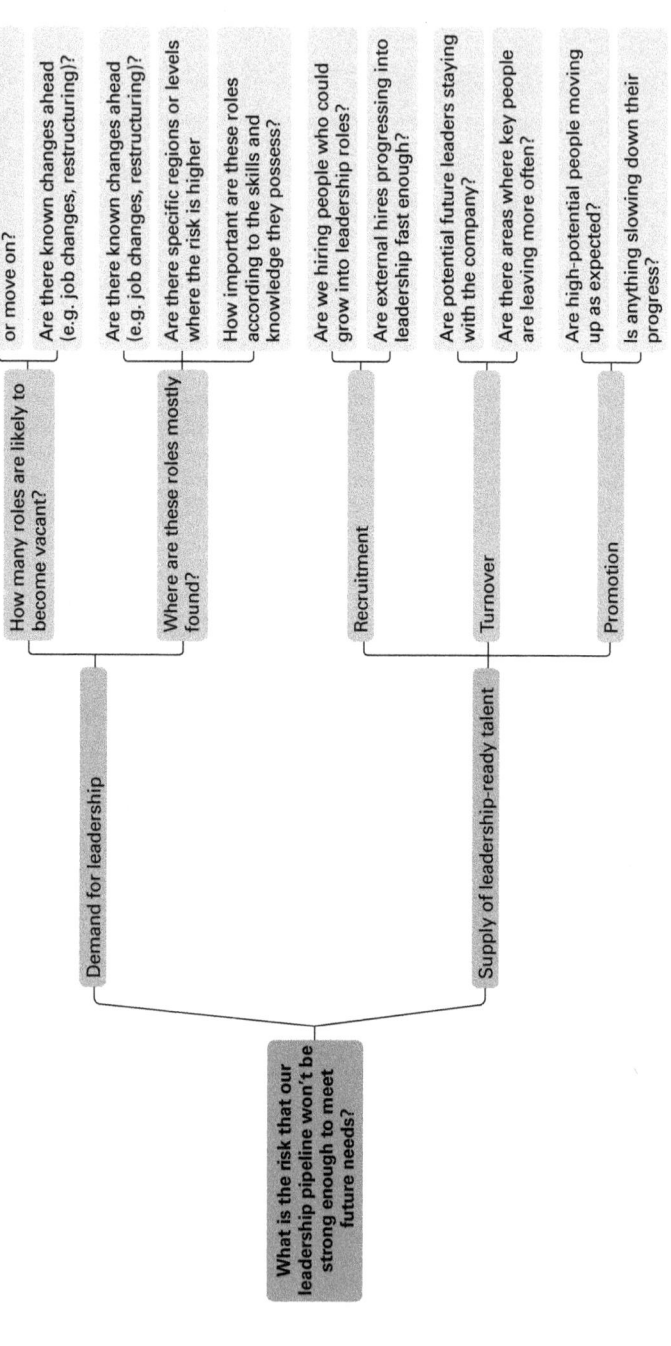

Scope management

With the issue tree mapped, it is time to move from framing to solving. But before diving into data, there is one crucial step: managing scope (refer to Chapter 1). Scope management here is about building and documenting shared clarity. What is in scope, what is out of scope and what could get in the way (what are the risks)?

WHAT WOULD YOU DO?
Number 13

Referring to our discussion about scope management in Chapter 1, if necessary, how would you outline the scope of your work for this project to Sakshi and Meredith? Remember to:

- Clarify the questions.

- Agree on what is needed.

- Surface risks.

Show how you would build the plan collaboratively and outline enough structure to keep the project on track, without being too rigid. Remember that it is not about ticking boxes. It is about trust, shared expectations and creating the space to deliver good work without surprises later.

Process mapping

Process mapping is one of the best ways to understand your business. In PA, it helps you uncover business context and data flow lineage. This becomes especially important when your analysis depends on operational processes that vary across teams or are mid-transition, which is the case in this scenario we are working with.

In this case, you are analysing internal leadership supply across two very different functions: sales and production. Before you can assess pipeline health, you need to understand how the data is captured, maintained and kept current. That means getting clear on the process behind the data. This is where process mapping comes in.

You do not need to be a process expert to get started. A simple flowchart that follows the input, process and output (IPO) steps is often enough to lay out the key steps. For succession planning, that might include when reviews happen, who identifies successors, and where updates are recorded. This gives you a basic structure to work from and helps you spot missing or unclear steps.

A tip is to position key decision points as steps and branch out the steps based on the decision made (similar to an issue tree) so you can see how the process and outcome vary and change based on the decision points.

Process mapping is particularly helpful to explain the business context behind the data. So when you later share your findings, you can say, 'Successor coverage in production appears higher, but the data is patchy because updates are not consistently recorded. In sales, the risk is greater because no formal process exists.' That kind of clarity helps your audience trust what they are seeing. It shows you are not just analysing data, but understanding how and why it came to be.

People frequently talk about needing to have 'business acumen' as a skill, but not many people can tell you how to build it. Process mapping and analysis can help you. The more business processes you map and understand, the more of the business you understand.

In the end, mapping gives you more than a visual. It helps you understand the problem deeply, so your analysis is not only accurate but grounded in how things actually work. It builds confidence in your work and opens the door to better, more informed decisions.

Process mapping can be as simple as a flow chart and as deep as a technical discipline, if you are interested in learning more, you can research this topic further.

CHAPTER SUMMARY

- Don't be tempted to jump into analysis until you fully understand the problem you've been asked to solve. Leading a discovery conversation and listening to the meaning behind what is said is one of the most important things you can do.

- Requests to PA are often based on a mix of assumptions that haven't been questioned before. Be sure to unpick these and check stakeholders agree with them before you delve in.

- Structuring the problem helps to clarify your thinking and define what needs testing. Use the MECE principle to break the problem down into distinct categories that cover as much of the issue as possible.

- The issue tree is another tool that helps you think and shape your hypotheses further.

- Process mapping is a useful tool to help you gain business acumen in areas that you are not familiar with.

REVIEW QUESTIONS

1 What are the different types of listening techniques?

2 If you are presented with an ambiguous problem, how could you clarify it and determine if it is yours to solve?

3 What's a good way to understand the business context you are working with quickly?

Endnotes

1 SurveyMonkey (2025) Comparing Closed-Ended and Open-Ended Questions, SurveyMonkey, www.surveymonkey.com/mp/comparing-closed-ended-and-open-ended-questions (archived at https://perma.cc/2QWJ-ZH8E)

2 Treasure, J (2020) Transform Your Relationships with Three Types of Listening, Julian Treasure, https://www.juliantreasure.com/blog/types-listening-relationships (archived at https://perma.cc/KFX3-M9LG)

3 Freedman, J L and Fraser, S C (1966) Compliance Without Pressure: The Foot-in-the-Door Technique, *Journal of Personality and Social Psychology*, 4(2), 195–202, https://psycnet.apa.org/doiLanding?doi=1 0.1037%2Fh0023552 (archived at https://perma.cc/DHP7-56QK)

4 Minto, B (nd) MECE: I Invented It, So I Get to Say How to Pronounce It, McKinsey & Company, 13 May, www.mckinsey.com/alumni/news-and-events/global-news/alumni-news/barbara-minto-mece-i-invented-it-so-i-get-to-say-how-to-pronounce-it (archived at https://perma.cc/69VK-URAT)

5 Minto, B (2009) *The Pyramid Principle: Logic in Writing and Thinking*, 3rd edn, Financial Times Prentice Hall

6 Chevallier, A (2016) *Strategic Thinking in Complex Problem Solving*, Oxford University Press

CHAPTER SEVEN

Data frameworks for people analytics

Introduction

This chapter contains the foundational data frameworks you need to understand to perform a people analytics project well. We cannot cover everything, but this chapter will give you the skeleton tools and language you need so you can keep learning on your own, with the right keywords, frameworks and mental models to explore deeper.

We begin by zooming out to look at the full analysis lifecycle, before breaking it down into the key stages: collecting and integrating data, doing the analysis and presenting insights clearly and persuasively.

Throughout, we'll return to the real-world example introduced in Chapter 6 of the leadership pipeline problem at the Japanese car manufacturer. Remember to check the Appendix for answers to the 'What would you do?' questions.

LEARNING OBJECTIVES

By the end of this chapter, you will be able to:

- Identify different types of data, and organize, clean and prepare it to make your analysis more reliable.

- Build sustainable data that can be reused, adapted and scaled.
- Describe different types of outputs you can achieve through your analysis and the methods to reach them.
- Explain some basic statistical terms such as distribution, hypothesis testing and regression.
- Choose the right chart to visualize your data and shape effective conversations.
- Craft structured stories with your data to encourage action.

Data analytics lifecycle

Every PA project moves through a cycle, starting with raw data and ending with insights that support decisions. This cycle has four main stages as outlined in Figure 7.1:

1 Data collection.
2 Data integration.
3 Data science.
4 Data visualization.

We'll run through each of these in turn.

Data collection

This involves gathering the data needed for your analysis. It might come from HR systems, surveys, spreadsheets or operational tools. Collecting data isn't just about getting the data files or data feed, it's about understanding how that data flows from the source, how often it's updated and who owns it. Process analysis (Chapter 7) matters here. The more you know the upstream systems and handovers, the easier it becomes to spot gaps, build trust in the data and automate later. If this analysis needs to be repeated, you will want to reduce manual effort by setting up reliable flows and clear documentation.

FIGURE 7.1   The people analytics lifecycle

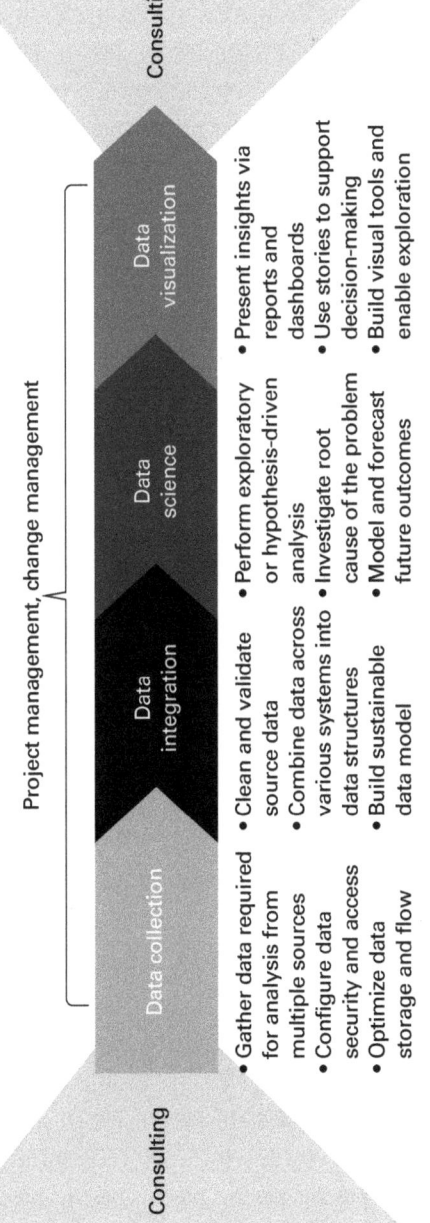

Project management, change management

Consulting

Data collection
- Gather data required for analysis from multiple sources
- Configure data security and access
- Optimize data storage and flow

Data integration
- Clean and validate source data
- Combine data across various systems into data structures
- Build sustainable data model

Data science
- Perform exploratory or hypothesis-driven analysis
- Investigate root cause of the problem
- Model and forecast future outcomes

Data visualization
- Present insights via reports and dashboards
- Use stories to support decision-making
- Build visual tools and enable exploration

Consulting

> In the leadership pipeline project, you will need to work with stakeholders to understand each data source's features, update frequency, limits and reliability. You may also need to set up templates, organize folders and agree on a sustainable way to receive the data, like self-service, emails or automated reports.

Data integration

Once you have collected the data, the next step is making it usable. This starts with cleaning it, fixing errors, standardizing formats and filling in or handling missing values. Then you move on to integrating it, which often means combining data from different systems, aligning naming conventions and resolving inconsistencies. The key here is efficiency. A well-structured integration process reduces confusion later, especially when you or someone else needs to revisit the analysis. That means creating clear, logical steps that are easy to trace and repeat, with documentation explaining how and why different sources were joined. Building a sustainable data model at the beginning can save a huge amount of time later.

> In your leadership pipeline project, this involves validating and aligning leadership data across production and sales to create a clear view of readiness by function and region.

Data science

This is where the actual analysis happens. To make sense of the data, it helps to have a working understanding of core statistics concepts. These basics help you spot patterns, compare and understand the strength and reliability of your findings. Depending on the question, you might use techniques like cohort analysis, trend comparisons over time or regression (these terms are explained later in the chapter). Some projects call for hypothesis testing, while others are more exploratory. You might also build simple models to predict future outcomes or identify key drivers behind a particular trend. The most important thing is choosing the right method for the problem you are trying to solve.

> In the leadership pipeline project, this means analysing future leadership demand and internal supply to bring structure to what started as a vague concern.

Data visualization

This is how you communicate what you found. It's where human-centred design (HCD) really matters (refer to Chapter 1). Good visualization is about understanding how people absorb information, what decisions they need to make and how to guide them through the data without overwhelming them. Dashboards, reports and visuals should highlight what matters most, using clear structure, plain language and thoughtful layout. Simplicity is powerful here. The best visuals help others see the story in the data, ask better questions and feel confident using it to make decisions.

> In your project, this is about delivering the agreed slide deck in a way that reflects both the sophistication of your analysis and the clarity of your storytelling, helping senior leaders quickly understand where action is needed.

Data collection and integration tools

Before you can dive into analysis or start building dashboards, you need to get your data sorted. This part of the work often feels like the least glamorous, but it is the most critical foundational step.

Understanding the environment your data is in

First, it's important to understand what kind of data you are working with, where it comes from and how it all connects. This helps to avoid confusion later and ensures you are working with the right information.

Start by identifying the data types in your dataset. These shape how you analyse and summarize the data:

- Categorical (or nominal): These are group labels with no specific order. Examples include position title, business unit or ethnicity. You can use counts or modes to summarize them.
- Ordinal: These are categories with a clear order, but the spacing between values may not be equal. A good example is performance ratings. You can rank them.
- Numerical (or quantitative): These are values you can measure or count, such as tenure, salary or number of training hours.
- Boolean: These are yes/no or true/false values, such as someone is a manager, completed training or eligibile for promotion.
- Date/time: Fields like birth date, hire date or training completion date.
- Text (free text): These are open-ended fields like survey comments or exit reasons.
- Key identifiers: Fields like employee ID, email address or user ID. These are unique values that help link records across systems.

With data coming from different systems, it helps to build a simple data dictionary. This is just a clear list of each field, what it means and how it's used. For example, is tenure calculated from hire date or most recent promotion?

To get a clearer view, sketch a quick data lineage diagram. This shows how data flows from original sources into your working file. It helps you spot duplicates, gaps or mismatches between systems.

You can also create a source system map to keep track of where each type of data lives.

One final thing to check: update frequency. Some systems refresh data quarterly, others update daily or in real time. Knowing this helps you avoid basing your insights on outdated information and lets you time your analysis to match the most up-to-date picture available.

Taking the time to organize and understand your data upfront will make your analysis more reliable. It can be hard work. Organizational data is often messy, scattered across systems or manually maintained. You may need to chase stakeholders, request access, dig through folders or clean inconsistent formats. It might feel like a lot of effort up front, but it is worth it. That early work gives you a clearer view of how things operate and helps you learn more about the organization than almost anything else.

ETL (extract, transform, load)

The next step is to pull the data together, clean it and prepare it for analysis. This process is often called ETL (Extract, Transform, Load),[1] and it is a skill frequently used in data analytics job descriptions:

- Extract means pulling data from the source, whether that's a system or a shared spreadsheet.
- Transform involves cleaning, reshaping and organizing the data so it's usable (this takes most of the effort).
- Load is the final step, getting your cleaned data into the format or tool where it is ready for you to analyse.

Three tools and concepts are especially useful here. SQL helps you extract and filter data directly from databases. The syntax (functions) is very simple which includes SELECT, FROM, WHERE, ORDER BY and many more, and a basic understanding can go a long way. Power Query (built into Excel and Power BI) lets you clean and transform data without code. It is ideal for handling messy spreadsheets or automating repetitive steps. You can use it to combine data from different sources or automate repetitive tasks like removing duplicates or filtering rows. Every step you take in Power Query is clearly shown in an ordered list on the side of the window so you can go back and change them or remove them if needed. This then acts as a template so the same steps can be repeated over and over without having to redo the steps.

And if you are pulling data from live systems or cloud platforms, understanding APIs is also important.

API (Application Programming Interface): A way for systems to talk to each other, allowing direct connection to a source system and real-time data retrieval, often through tools like Python, Postman or Power BI connectors. APIs are especially helpful when working with systems that update regularly or when you want to avoid manual downloads.

SQL (Structured Query Language): A language you can use to speak with the database to extract the specific data you want. You can use simple English commands like SELECT to determine which columns to bring in, FROM to allow you to specify the database and WHERE to allow you to apply filter conditions. You can use SQL not only to get data from the database but also update the database (if you have write access to the database).

WHAT WOULD YOU DO?
Number 14

Think about the data you will need to collect for the leadership pipeline project:

- How will you receive the data and what tool might be helpful?
- How will you clean the data, and what tool could you use?
- What issues do you anticipate needing to fix in the data?
- Where will most of your energy need to go?

Governance, security and trust

As PA professionals, we are frequently exposed to extremely sensitive data. In the real-world example project, that means handling leadership and succession information with care, following clear processes and approaching the work with a mindset of data stewardship. Datasets including names, ratings or talent flags mean that you are dealing with information that has regulatory consequences. Mishandling it, even unintentionally, can erode trust and put the organization at risk.

One of the priorities is managing access and permissions. In the real-world example, you would connect with system owners to gain access to succession and training records, follow internal protocols for approvals and avoid storing personal information in unsecured folders.

Data masking is another key part of working responsibly. This means hiding or replacing identifying details, like names or employee IDs, so that individuals are not easily recognized.

To stay organized, use version control and change tracking. Files follow a clear naming pattern and keep a simple changelog that notes what changed and why.

Before presenting any findings, you should run basic data quality checks with a stakeholder to make sure more than one pair of eyes has checked the findings.

WHAT WOULD YOU DO?
Number 15

With the leadership pipeline project, what would you ask a stakeholder to look out for in the data quality check?

Sustainable data integration

One of the biggest systems thinking mindset shifts is learning to design not just for today's problem, but for tomorrow's as well. Much of our work in people analytics is not a one-off. It gets reused, adapted and scaled. The earlier you start thinking with long-term sustainability in mind, the more value your work brings over time. It's about understanding how data moves between platforms, how often it's needed, who uses it and where it might be reused. It is not just a mindset; it has a practical impact.

In your leadership pipeline project, you combined succession data, training records and other inputs to assess future leadership supply. That dataset cannot only be used for a strategic conversation today, but it can also become a foundation for future use. With a bit of foresight, it can support analysis on promotion pathways, mobility or diversity. Build it well once today, and it can save many people many hours later.

Start with standardization. Clean, consistent lookup tables for job levels, functions or regions make it far easier to join new datasets down the line. Today, you are merging LMS completions. Tomorrow, it might be recruitment or performance data. Standardized references reduce rework and make your data models more flexible.

Then there's scalability. Your process should work whether it covers 100 or 10,000 people. Avoid manual edits. Use structured queries and repeatable steps. Test your model at different sizes and scopes. Could it run across multiple regions? Can it flex for more than just one unit? A solid model should scale with minimal effort.

Reusability and documentation also matter. In Power Query, keep steps clear. In SQL, comment your code and organize it logically. Save both raw and cleaned versions of your data. Write a summary explaining your process. Whether it's for a teammate or the future you, anyone should be able to pick up the work and understand what was done.

Finally, think about automation. Once your process is reliable, explore ways to make it run on its own. Set Power Query to refresh when new files land in a shared folder. Schedule SQL jobs to feed dashboards weekly. Use tools like Power Automate or timed notifications or alerts to stay updated. Automation does not need to be complex, but it should reduce manual work and boost consistency.

Data science frameworks

Data science can seem technical and overwhelming, but you don't need to know everything to work effectively in people analytics. A disclaimer: this section will not teach you how to build models or write code. Often, you don't need to know how to use many of these tools. You just need to know what they are for, what to Google and when to bring in experts. There are also many books on the market that deep dive into predictive PA.

This section gives you a clear view of the types of analysis you might use, the kinds of insights they produce and how they connect to real-world problems.

To keep things simple, we will use the IPO model. At this point in your leadership pipeline project, you already have the input: a cleaned, integrated dataset. The goal is to get to the output, which is the insights you want to deliver to answer the questions laid out earlier using the issue tree.

Output – the types of insights you can deliver

The outcomes that we can achieve through analysis can typically be classified into the following groups:

1 Trends – How have things changed over time?
2 Variances – Where are the biggest differences?
3 Relationships and drivers – What factors are linked to outcomes?
4 Root causes – Why is this happening?
5 Segments or clusters – What distinct groups exist?
6 Predictions – What is likely to happen next?
7 Forecasts – What will the numbers look like in the future?
8 Time-to-event estimates – When will something happen?
9 Recommended actions – What should we do to get the outcome we want?

Process – how do you get to these insights?

Achieving the output requires a range of different methods. The list below gives them in order from the most to least frequently used, to give you an idea of which skills are most practical:

- Time series analysis: Looking at data points across time to see if something is increasing, decreasing or cyclical.
- Exploratory data analysis (EDA): A first look at the data, scanning for patterns, totals, averages or anything that stands out.
- Aggregation and summary statistics: Grouping data by time period (e.g. by quarter) and calculating metrics like average, total or percentage.
- Cross-tabulation and pivoting: Creating a table that compares two variables, for example, job level by region and summarizes what's happening in each group.
- Variance and segmentation: Breaking data into segments (like function or level) and comparing numbers between them.

- Cohort analysis: Tracking a specific group over time. For example, tracking successors added in 2022 to see how long it took them to become 'leadership ready'.
- Forecasting models: Tools that project numbers into the future using historical trends (e.g. headcount, readiness supply).
- Comparative drilldowns: Starting with a big group (like all successors) and drilling down to smaller groups (like site, department, manager) to find where the difference lies.
- Correlation analysis: A simple way to test whether two things tend to move together, such as training hours and readiness level.
- Regression analysis: A more formal method to measure how much one factor (or several) affects an outcome. You could use it to estimate how much training increases the likelihood of being 'leadership ready'
- Hypothesis testing: A method to test if a difference you saw (e.g. between departments) is meaningful or just random.
- Clustering: A technique that groups people automatically based on patterns in the data.
- Machine learning classification models: These models predict categories, for example, 'high potential' or 'not ready'. They use past data to learn patterns and apply them to current employees.
- Survival analysis: This helps predict when something will happen, like resignation or promotion, by modelling time-to-event.[2]
- Optimization techniques: Used when you have constraints (like budget) and need to find the best solution across options. This can be done via Excel's inbuilt functionality.

Integrating methods and outcomes

The nine outcomes listed previously can typically be achieved by integrating certain processes.

TRENDS

- Time series analysis
- Exploratory data analysis (EDA)
- Aggregation and summary statistics
- Cohort analysis

VARIANCES

- Variance and segmentation
- Cross-tabulation and pivoting
- Comparative drilldowns
- EDA

RELATIONSHIPS AND DRIVERS

- Correlation analysis
- Regression analysis
- EDA

ROOT CAUSES

- Comparative drilldowns
- Hypothesis testing
- Correlation and regression

SEGMENTS AND CLUSTERS

- Clustering
- Cohort analysis
- Dimensionality reduction
- EDA

PREDICTIONS

- Classification models
- Regression analysis
- Survival analysis
- Forecasting models

FORECASTS

- Forecasting models
- Time series analysis
- Regression analysis
- Survival analysis

TIME-TO-EVENT ESTIMATES

- Survival analysis
- Cohort analysis
- Regression analysis

RECOMMENDED ACTIONS

- Optimization techniques

Statistics foundation

Executives often use statistical terms to test credibility, validate insight quality or simply signal that they are paying attention. Sometimes they understand the terms, and sometimes... they just know they are supposed to ask.

As you move from standard reporting into deeper analysis, it's helpful to get familiar with the kinds of statistical terms that start showing up in questions and conversations. These might be mentioned in meetings, used in dashboards or dropped into a quick challenge from a senior stakeholder who's trying to test the quality of your thinking.

This section gives you a grounding in the core statistics terms you will hear most often in people analytics, grouped into three key areas:

1 Distribution and shape of data.
2 Hypothesis testing.
3 Regression and modelling.

Distribution and shape of data

When you're working with data about people, such as salaries and performance scores, not everything is neat and symmetrical (like height). Some values lean heavily to one side. That's where skewness comes in.[3]

Skewness shows whether your data is lopsided. For example, if most people earn between £25,000 and £40,000 but a few earn over £100,000, the data is positively (right) skewed. Vice versa, if most people earn over £100,000 with a few earning between £25,000 and £40,000, the data is negatively (left) skewed. That long tail of high earners pulls the average up. In cases like this, the mean can be misleading. The median, or middle value, usually gives a better idea of what's typical. This brings us to the three main types of averages:

- The mean is the total of all values divided by the number of entries. This is the traditional sense of average, when you add everything together and divide by the count. Use it when your data is balanced.
- The median is the middle value when the data is in order. Use it when your data is skewed or has outliers (we discuss outliers below). In cases where there's an even number of values, you take the average of the middle two values.
- The mode is the value that appears most often. Use it when looking for things like job level or department. It's important to note that there can be more than one mode or no mode at all depending on the data.

To understand how varied your data is, look at the minimum and maximum values first. These tell you the lowest and highest points. But they don't show the full picture.

Standard deviation gives you a sense of how tightly values surround the mean. A small standard deviation means people are quite similar. A large one means there's more variation. Variance is closely related. It also measures spread, but it's the average of the squared differences from the mean. It comes up more in formal statistical tests, but the concept is the same.

If your data is evenly spread around the mean, it may follow a normal distribution. This is the classic bell curve, where most people fall near the middle and fewer are at the extremes. A lot of statistical methods assume this shape, but many real-world datasets (especially in HR) are not perfectly normal. Therefore, it is important to understand the concept and calculations that will help you check the distribution.[4]

Finally, watch out for outliers. These are extreme values that don't fit the pattern. One or two very unusual scores can throw off your averages and make your data look more spread out than it really is. It's a good idea to flag them and see how your results change with and without them.

Learning and understanding how these pieces fit together helps you make better decisions.

Hypothesis testing – does a difference matter?

When working with people data, it's not enough to just notice a pattern or difference. You need to check whether that difference is real or if it might have happened by chance. That's where hypothesis testing and statistical significance come in.

Every test begins with a null hypothesis. This is the default assumption that there is no real difference or effect. For example, if you compare engagement scores between two departments, the null hypothesis says the scores are the same.

The alternative hypothesis suggests the opposite – there is a meaningful difference or relationship. In most cases, your goal is to gather enough evidence to reject the null hypothesis and support the alternative.[5]

To do this, you can use a significance test. This tells you whether the difference you are seeing is likely to be real. Most tests give you a p-value. If that value is less than 0.05,[6] the result is usually considered statistically significant. In other words, there is a strong chance the difference is real, not random.

Your results are only as reliable as the data behind them, which is why sample size is important. This refers to how many people or data points are included in your analysis. A group size of 30 or more is a good rule of thumb when comparing averages. Smaller groups may not give stable or trustworthy results.[7]

Here are a few common tests you may come across:[8]

- T-test: Compares the average of two groups. For example, is the average readiness score in Sales lower than in Engineering? Works best with numerical data and groups of 30 or more people.
- Variance testing: Looks at how spread out the data is in each group. This helps you see if one team has more consistency in scores than another, even if the averages are similar. It's useful for understanding stability in things like manager ratings or engagement.
- Chi-square test: Compares two categorical variables. For instance, is there a link between job level and readiness status, or between gender and promotion outcomes? This helps you work out whether the pattern you see is likely to be meaningful.

Hypothesis testing gives you a way to back up your insights with evidence. It helps you move from observations to trusted conclusions, which is key when sharing findings with leaders or making decisions based on data.

Here it's important to highlight the difference between a business hypothesis and a statistical hypothesis. You will hear the word 'hypothesis' a lot. Most of the time, people will be talking about a business hypothesis. A business hypothesis is a practical idea or assumption you want to explore and test framed around business goals or observations, for example, you might hear 'My hypothesis is that when employees are working from home, they are more likely to get burnt out'. This is a business hypothesis, it's a starting point for inquiry, not a formal test. The key is to recognize it for what it is, and translate it to a statistical hypothesis later if needed.

Regression and modelling

Regression and modelling help you understand patterns and predict outcomes.[9] Once you have tested for differences in your data, you might want to understand relationships, make predictions or explore what factors are driving outcomes.

Before jumping into models, it's important to understand the difference between correlation and causation. Correlation means two things move together. For example, if people who complete more training are more likely to be promoted, that's a correlation. But that doesn't mean one causes the other. Causation means that one variable directly affects another. Unless you have run a controlled experiment or have strong supporting evidence, it's safer to say that things are related rather than claiming one causes the other.[10]

Regression is a tool that helps you explore these relationships more deeply. The simplest form is linear regression, which looks at how one or more variables predict a continuous outcome, like performance score or tenure. For example, you might look at how training hours and job level relate to engagement scores.

When your outcome is a yes/no or true/false question, such as whether someone was promoted or completed onboarding, you would use logistic regression. This helps you estimate the likelihood of an outcome happening based on different factors.

Often, you will want to include several factors at once. That's where multivariable regression comes in. It allows you to control for other influences and get a clearer picture of which factors really matter. For instance, you might find that training appears linked to high engagement, but once you control for job level and tenure, the effect disappears, revealing the true drivers of engagement.

If you are working with time-based outcomes, like how long someone stays at the company or how long it takes to complete a course, survival analysis is useful. It's especially helpful when not everyone in your dataset has experienced the outcome yet. One common method here is Cox regression, which shows how different variables affect the chance of something happening over time, such as resignation risk.

Once the model is set up, you want to understand how well it performs. R-squared, often written as R^2, tells you how much of the variation in your outcome is explained by your model. A higher value means the model fits the data well, while a lower value suggests there's still a lot the model doesn't capture.[11]

Regression and modelling let you move from describing your data to explaining it and even predicting what might happen next. Used thoughtfully, they can help you answer complex questions, test ideas and provide evidence for people decisions.

Data visualization

Once you have done the hard part to uncover insights, you are ready to put pen to paper to show them to your stakeholders. This is where data visualization becomes your most valuable tool. The best visuals do not just present findings, they guide thinking. They help leaders spot the issue, feel the urgency and know exactly where to act. When done right, a chart becomes less about numbers and more about meaning. And the trick is this: it should feel like their idea. Your role is to tee it up clearly and let them connect the dots.

TOP TIP

Make your stakeholders feel smart

Avoid a mistake that a lot of beginners make. Do not use data visualization to show how smart you are. Use it to make your stakeholders feel smart, like they were the ones who figured it out.

Let's go back to the leadership pipeline case. You could say, '38% of senior leaders in Production are retiring within three years.' Or you could show it. A bar chart with Production highlighted, titled 'Production faces the highest leadership risk', lets the data speak. It's fast, focused and immediately shows where attention is needed.

One good chart can cut through the noise, shape a conversation and lead to action. Here is how to create them.

Choosing the right medium for the job

A frequently mixed up concept is which tool to present the data in. Just because you have built a visually impressive dashboard using tools like Power BI or Tableau, it doesn't mean sharing the dashboard will automatically land the insights with your audience. If the purpose is to tell the story, then it needs to be delivered in a storytelling format.

Dashboards are powerful for exploration, monitoring and repeated insights. But when it comes to communicating a message, especially to senior stakeholders, a structured narrative presented clearly and intentionally is far more effective. That's where presentation tools like PowerPoint, Google Slides or Canva come in. These tools allow you to control the flow of information, highlight what matters and build a compelling argument slide by slide.

Choosing the right chart for the job

Once you've decided on the right medium, it's time to choose the right chart. There's no perfect chart, but some types work better for certain messages. Use this list as a quick guide to choosing the right one:

- Compare across dimensions – bar chart.
- Show changes over time – line chart.
- Show distribution or spread – column chart/histogram or box plot.
- Highlight key numbers – big callout number/KPI.
- Show status or coverage – table with colour coding.
- Show parts of a whole – donut chart or tree map.

Pro tips for effective visualizations

Good visualization isn't about showing everything, it is about showing the right thing in the clearest possible way. A great chart helps someone instantly see what matters and feel confident about what to do next. Here are key principles (and a few pro tricks) to keep your charts focused, actionable and easy to understand based on the work of Edward Tufte[12] and Stephen Few:[13]

1 **Start with purpose**
   Begin with the one message you want your audience to take away. If they forget everything else, what should they remember? Design the entire visual around that idea. If the chart needs a lot of explanation, it's not ready yet.

2 **Highlight what matters**
   Draw attention to the most important part of the chart using colour, bold text or size, but just one of them. A good trick is to mute everything else in a neutral tone (like grey), so your key insight pops. Let the visual lead the conversation.

3 **Remove the noise**
   Strip out anything that adds clutter or confusion, such as extra gridlines, 3D effects, drop shadows or decorative elements. Don't make people work to interpret your work. If you included clear data labels, consider removing axis labels altogether. Think like a minimalist: every element should earn its place.

4 **Respect how people read and process visuals**
   Follow a logical left-to-right, top-to-bottom reading order. Put time on the horizontal axis. Arrange categories in a sensible sequence. Stick with common conventions, such as red for risk and green for positive and use consistent formats so your audience doesn't have to keep re-learning how to read your charts.

5 **Use faceting to compare clearly**
   Faceting means breaking a complex chart into smaller, side-by-side versions that show different slices of the data, like

one chart per team, site or time period. This reduces clutter while making comparisons easier. If you are comparing readiness across three departments, three clean mini charts (using the same scale and layout) are often clearer than one busy chart with lots of colours and categories competing for space.

6   **Use colour with care**
Stick to a simple palette, one highlight colour, one neutral and one contextual if needed. Avoid using more than three at once. Always check for accessibility, avoiding red-green combinations (which can be difficult for people with colour vision deficiency) and ensuring there's enough contrast for all users (as some users can struggle to see different shades of the same colour). Use patterns or labels when needed to make visuals readable for everyone.

7   **Keep visuals clean, move detail to footnotes or appendices**
If the chart is doing its job, it shouldn't need every piece of context on the slide. Use a footnote for definitions, data sources or filters. Move detailed breakdowns or deeper analysis into an appendix. This keeps your main visuals clean and focused, while still giving curious or analytical viewers a place to dig deeper.

8   **Title your chart like a headline, not a label**
Instead of 'Leadership readiness by function', use 'Sales leadership pipeline lags behind other teams'. Your title should tell the audience what to look for and why it matters. A good headline sets the frame and directs attention, it makes the visual's purpose clear before they even look at the data.

Remember that your chart isn't there to impress. It's there to direct attention to what you want your stakeholders to think and see, so the action feels obvious. When a stakeholder looks at your slide and says, 'We need to do something about that' your visual has done its job.

Data storytelling

So, you have collected the data, run the analysis and uncovered something meaningful. But insight alone doesn't shift behaviour. Data storytelling makes change feel possible.

Storytelling in people analytics is about helping people see that a problem exists that needs to be acted on. It helps leaders make sense of what needs to change, in a way that feels natural and safe to act on. The biggest blocker is often resistance to what the data implies – that things need to be done differently.

In this section, you will learn how to combine the consulting skills discussed in Chapter 6 and analysis skills into storytelling techniques that help translate your insights into action.

Presentation frameworks: crafting structured stories

Having a good story is only half the job. The other half is delivering it in a format your audience can digest, especially under time pressure. Consultants use structured frameworks to organize thoughts clearly and persuasively. Here are three essential ones to know.

MINTO PYRAMID PRINCIPLE

The Minto Pyramid Principle is one of the most effective ways to structure your message. It was developed by Barbara Minto at McKinsey for time-poor decision-makers who want to hear the answer first, not at the end after a tour through your entire process. The idea is simple: start with the conclusion, support it with key reasons and finish with evidence. Imagine building a pyramid from the top down. It gives your audience immediate clarity, backed by logic and data.[14] It also helps you sharpen your thinking. If you cannot clearly state your main message at the top, you probably need to rethink it.

> **TOP TIP**
> Get to the 'so-what' fast
>
> As an early-career professional, get into the habit of leading with the 'so what'. It's one of the fastest ways to stand out.

SCQA: SITUATION, COMPLICATION, QUESTION, ANSWER

If the pyramid is all about getting to the point, SCQA, which stands for Situation, Complication, Question and Answer and was also invented by Barbara Minto at McKinsey, helps you set the stage. It gives structure to the story behind your analysis so your audience understands why the topic matters before you deliver your answer.[15]

You can use SCQA to open a presentation, write a compelling summary or frame a proposal. It works well because it mirrors how people naturally think. It creates structure without rushing to the conclusion, making it ideal when you need to introduce a problem and build shared understanding.

> **WHAT WOULD YOU DO?**
> Number 16
>
> Use Minto's SCQA framework to outline the situation (current state), complication (problem), key question that needs to be answered and the answer for the leadership pipeline project.

ABT: AND, BUT, THEREFORE

Sometimes you do not need a full framework. You just need one punchy sentence that sets the scene, builds tension and lands the point. That is where ABT comes in, which stands for And, But, Therefore, and was developed by biologist Randy Olson.[16] It is perfect for slide openers, status updates, emails or check-ins with busy stakeholders. You start by describing the current state (And), then introduce the problem (But), and finally explain what you are doing about it (Therefore). For example, for the leadership pipeline project, you could say, 'We reviewed succession coverage and forecasted retirement risk across divisions, but only three out of five critical roles have internal successors. Therefore, we are recommending targeted promotion and development planning.' ABT is quick, clear and confident. It is especially effective when you want to show that you have already thought things through.

Managing tension, the key to a good story

Tension/pressure point is one of the simplest ways to make your data compelling.[17] When everything sounds fine, people tune out. But show that something is off or might go off track and you have their attention. It's the shift from 'nice to know' to 'we need to act'. Tension creates contrast. It highlights a gap between where things are and where they should be.[18] It's the reason your data matters in the first place.

HOW TO BUILD TENSION

To build tension, start with contrast. Set up the current state, then show how it could be better. For example, 'Only 60% of our ready-now talent is being promoted within two years, but with a structured development plan, that could rise to 85%.' You've turned a number into a problem with potential.

Another strong approach is to surface what's at stake. Spell out what happens if nothing changes. What will the business lose? What's the missed opportunity? If a pattern continues, what will it cost us in six months? This doesn't have to be overly dramatic, just clear. 'If turnover among successors stays this high, we risk losing key talent before they can step up.'

You can also break a pattern. People notice when something that used to be stable suddenly shifts. Maybe a team has always had high engagement, and now it's dropped. Maybe your promotion pipeline has always been strong, and suddenly, it isn't. Those moments get attention because they disrupt expectations.

Be specific. Vagueness is forgettable. Numbers that feel sharp and real cut through faster. '12% of mid-level hires entered the succession plan' is much more effective than 'a small percentage'. Specificity builds credibility and makes your insight harder to ignore.

And finally, give it a name. When a problem has a label, people remember it. Even a touch of humour or metaphor can go a long way.

HOW TO RESOLVE TENSION

Once you have built tension by highlighting a challenge or gap, bring your audience into the resolution to ease the tension. This is where insight becomes impact. By co-creating the path forward, you turn observation into action together.

Start by shaping a clear recommendation, not in isolation, but as a starting point for shared thinking. Don't hedge with five equal options. Instead, suggest a direction based on the evidence: 'We recommend prioritizing internal promotions for critical roles, while using short-term coverage for others.' Be confident, but invite feedback: 'This is where the data points us, what are your thoughts so far?'

If there are multiple paths, surface them, but guide the group towards the most promising one. Anchor your point of view with openness: 'There are three viable options, but based on what we know so far, internal promotion appears to be the strongest path. How do you feel about this?'

Support your suggestion with a few sharp data points that resonate. Keep it concise: '60% of leadership talent has already been promoted within two years, which suggests the pipeline can support this shift.' This gives the group something real to react to, affirm or build on.

Then, frame the resolution as forward momentum. Show that the challenge isn't a dead-end, but something we can address together.

Finally, visualize the answer, together. A clear, simple chart or side-by-side view can unite the group around a shared understanding. Show before and after. Show risk and resolution. Pair it with a focused title that invites discussion. A strong visual gives the team something to align around and act on.

Insights co-creation: the secret recipe to success

One of the fastest ways to turn a decent analysis into something people use is also the one we often skip: co-creation.[19] It's not about handing over a shiny finished product and hoping someone reads it. It's about inviting others into the insight process. You let them poke at the data, ask questions and shape the meaning with you. When people help build the story, they are far more likely to act on it, because it feels like theirs.

TOP TIP
Ditch the expert burden

In PA, there's a quiet pressure to have the answers. You got the dashboards, the model, the stats. You must know, right? But here's the truth: certainty is overrated.

You are working with human behaviour, which isn't normally distributed. It's messy, inconsistent and shaped by variables that aren't captured in your system.

You are not here to explain the world. You are here to surface useful patterns, test hypotheses and invite stakeholders into a conversation that's informed by data, but not limited to it.

Real insight doesn't often come from being 'right', but from knowing what to ask next. The best analysts aren't perfect predictors, they are curious guides. Shifting from the explainer to the collaborator takes the pressure off and makes your work more powerful.

CO-CREATE THE INSIGHT TOGETHER IN LOOPS

In a PA role, you will frequently find yourself with incomplete but interesting data. A trend without a clear cause. A gap without context. That's your invitation to co-create. Share what you are seeing, then ask others what they see in it, too. Ask what might be missing, what's surprising or what feels off. When you do this early and often, you end up with a story that's richer, more grounded and much more likely to lead to action.

Co-creation means working iteratively. Instead of polishing something in isolation and revealing it all at once, you share early, gather feedback and shape the insight together. It keeps you close to the real problem and the people who need to solve it. The goal isn't to be finished, it's to be useful. And when you build with others, your work becomes something they trust and take forward.

BALANCE ASK AND TELL

Great insight work is about engaging. You need both asking and telling in your toolkit. Too much telling, and you sound like you are lecturing. Too much to asking, and people lose direction. Start by sharing what the data is showing, then ask for perspective. Offer a point of view but invite others to shape it. This balance keeps the conversation grounded in evidence while creating space for judgement, context and experience to play their part.

Co-creation deepens your work. You are not giving away ownership. You are building buy-in. And that's what turns analysis into action: insight that people believe in because they helped create it.

CHAPTER SUMMARY

- The data analytics lifecycle consists of four stages: data collection, integration, science and visualization.
- It's critical to sort and understand your data before progressing with the analysis. This can be laborious, but skipping it might make your analysis unreliable.
- Give your work a lasting impact by designing data so that it can be reused to solve future problems. Standardize it, and

make it scalable and reusable. Document processes and automate what you can.

- Outcomes can typically be classified into nine groups, which are achieved by integrating different processes and methods.

- You don't need to be a statistics genius, but aim to know enough to answer any questions stakeholders might throw at you.

- Data visualization is about choosing the right chart to shape conversations and show leaders how they need to act.

- Use frameworks like the Pyramid Principle, SCQA and ABT to make clear recommendations fast.

REVIEW QUESTIONS

1   Think about a recent analytics project you completed, how does it fit into the analytics lifecycle?

2   List three things you should keep in mind to integrate data sustainably.

3   How can you make your data visualization more impactful?

Endnotes

1   IBM (2025) What Is ETL (Extract, Transform, Load)?, IBM, https://www.ibm.com/topics/etl (archived at https://perma.cc/4QRU-987H)

2   Schober, P and Vetter, T R (2018) Survival Analysis and Interpretation of Time-to-Event Data: The Tortoise and the Hare, *Anesth Analg*, 127(3), 792–798, https://pubmed.ncbi.nlm.nih.gov/30015653 (archived at https://perma.cc/Y935-5VGF)

3   Bulmer, M G (1979) *Principles of Statistics*, Dover Publications

4   Agresti, A and Finlay, B (2017) *Statistical Methods for the Social Sciences*, 5th edn, Pearson

5   Price, P C, Jhangiani, R S and Chiang, I A (2015) Research Methods in Psychology, 2nd Canadian edn, BCcampus, https://opentextbc.ca/researchmethods (archived at https://perma.cc/8ZAG-TA7H)

6   Cohen, J (1994) World Is Round (p < .05), *American Psychologist*,
     49, 997–1003 https://doi.org/10.1037/0003-066X.49.12.997
     (archived at https://perma.cc/6P5Q-BB9J)

7   Roscoe, J T (1975) *Fundamental Research Statistics for the
     Behavioral Science*, International Series in Decision Process, 2nd edn,
     Holt, Rinehart and Winston, Inc

8   Moore, D S, McCabe, G P and Craig, B A (2016) *Introduction to the
     Practice of Statistics*, W H Freeman and Company

9   Triola, M F (2018) *Elementary Statistics*, 13th edn, Pearson

10 JMP (2025) Correlation vs Causation: Introduction to Statistics,
     https://www.jmp.com/en_us/statistics-knowledge-portal/what-is-
     correlation/correlation-vs-causation.html (archived at https://perma.cc/
     7C98-F6G3)

11 Triola, M F (2018) *Elementary Statistics*, 13th edn, Pearson, https://
     www.pearson.com/en-us/subject-catalog/p/elementary-statistics/P200
     000007465/9780134463063?srsltid=AfmBOookjm0w1g4VrJMos7U
     rq8u7n-aWLY9IwaT7NMv0VrZ1dhw615ts (archived at
     https://perma.cc/BT8Z-WNPS)

12 Tufte, E R (2001) *The Visual Display of Quantitative Information*,
     2nd edn, Graphics Press

13 Few, S (2009) *Now You See It: Simple Visualization Techniques for
     Quantitative Analysis*, Analytics Press

14 Minto, B (1996) *The Minto Pyramid Principle: Logic in Writing,
     Thinking and Problem Solving*, Minto Books

15 Minto, B (2009) *The Pyramid Principle: Logic in Writing and
     Thinking*, 3rd edn, Financial Times Prentice Hall

16 Olson, R (2015) *Houston, We Have a Narrative: Why Science Needs
     Story*, University of Chicago Press

17 Arrowsmith, S (2024) *Pressure Point: The Crucial Role of Conflict in
     Data Storytelling*, GreenBook, www.greenbook.org/insights/
     grow-your-insights-business/pressure-point-the-crucial-role-of-
     conflict-in-data-storytelling (archived at https://perma.cc/L56T-K86P)

18 Knaflic, C N (2023) *Identifying Tension in Data Stories*, Storytelling
     with Data, www.storytellingwithdata.com/blog/identifying-tension-
     in-data-stories (archived at https://perma.cc/D5TL-TTVG)

19 LinkedIn (2025) How Do You Ensure the Quality and Relevance of
     Insights?, https://www.linkedin.com/advice/1/how-do-you-ensure-
     quality-relevance-insights (archived at https://perma.cc/48T6-XVVL)

CHAPTER EIGHT

Successful people analytics translation

Introduction

At this stage, you should have a general understanding of how you can transform input to output in people analytics by going through the process of analysis and synthesis. Now, we will finish building the foundation by looking at the essential context you need to know when executing people analytics in an organization. This includes common problems that different functional areas within and outside of HR will bring to you, business buzzwords and acronyms you need to understand so you don't get sidetracked in meetings. We also consider how to overcome some difficult situations, such as conflict, resistance and unreasonable deterrents.

Understanding and applying the knowledge in this chapter will give you the kind of advantage that typically comes through years of experience or insider knowledge.

LEARNING OBJECTIVES

By the end of this chapter, you will be able to:

- Identify and categorize common PA problems across time, mobility and capability dimensions.

- Understand structured approaches to slicing data (by time, demographics and employment attributes) to generate richer, more actionable insights.

- Recognize and respond to synthesis challenges such as low disclosure, data quality issues and organizational barriers to trust.

- Select appropriate tools and platforms for analysis, balancing technical capability with audience needs and business context.

- Navigate difficult stakeholder behaviours and high-stakes conversations using practical, psychology-informed strategies that build influence and trust.

Common problems you might encounter

Here are some frequently asked questions you are likely to be asked in a PA role. This list is by no means exhaustive, and the problems we solve are constantly evolving as the technology we work with develops.

Problems related to analysis

Most analysis challenges fall into a few big buckets. For these problems, your work will often focus on breaking down existing data to spot issues, patterns or risks. Getting familiar with them early on saves you a lot of time later. To keep things clear, we will use three handy dimensions: time, mobility and capability. Think of these as lenses to understand where the organization is thriving and struggling.

TIME – HOW LONG DO THINGS TAKE?

- Time to hire/offer/establish productivity for new hires – How quickly the organization can bring candidates through the hiring stages and get them productive.
- Time for competence in training – How quickly employees become fully trained in any subject area.
- Learning completion rates – How many employees finish required or optional learning programmes within a given time.
- Recruitment application conversion rates – How many applicants move through stages like application to offer acceptance, or application to hire.
- Recruitment funnel analysis – Breaks down each step of the hiring journey (applications, screenings, interviews, offers) to find bottlenecks or drop-off points.
- SLA fulfilment/time to resolve – Whether HR services, such as case management or routine tasks, are being completed within agreed times.
- Time to adopt new process/technology – How quickly employees start using new systems, policies or tools after launch.
- Employee tenure – Length of time employees stay with the organization.
- Time to promote/progress – How long it takes employees to earn promotions or role progressions.
- Productivity lost due to absenteeism – How much productivity is lost because of unplanned absences.
- Time in role – How long employees typically stay in the same position before moving on or up.

MOBILITY – HOW DO PEOPLE MOVE INTERNALLY AND EXTERNALLY?

- Voluntary/involuntary turnover analysis – Why people leave the organization, either by choice or due to business decisions.
- Vacancy rate – Proportion of roles that are unfilled at a point in time relative to total headcount.

- Promotion rate – How many employees move up into higher-level positions.
- Internal mobility rate – How often employees move laterally or upward within the company.
- Internal training participation – Volume of employees engaged with internal learning opportunities.
- Career development analysis – Whether employees are being supported to grow their careers inside the organization through upwards/cross-functional movements and learning.
- High potential/performer leakage – Loss rate of top talent.
- Leadership pipeline size – How many employees are ready to step into leadership roles.
- External candidate size – The size and health of the organization's external talent pools.
- Contingent workforce pipeline size – The supply of temporary workers available.
- Hire/promotion/exit rates – The percentage of hiring, promotions and exits relative to the overall workforce.
- Headcount planning – Estimate future headcount needs based on supply and demand.
- Income disparity/pay gap analysis – Differences in earnings across groups (such as gender, ethnicity, job level or location) to identify and address unequal pay patterns.

CAPABILITY – WHO MOVES AND WHY?

- Headcount forecast waterfall – Waterfall chart showing expected headcount changes over time (hires, exits, transfers) to explain workforce growth or shrinkage.
- Workforce diversity – The representation of different groups across the organization.
- Employee experience/engagement metrics – Employee sentiment and satisfaction through surveys, feedback platforms or engagement scores.

- Skill gap heatmap – Visualizes where current workforce skills meet, exceed or fall short of future business needs.
- Incentive programme/benefit utilization – How many employees make use of bonuses, recognition schemes or other reward and benefit programmes.
- Overtime cost analysis – How much is being spent on overtime work.
- Manager effectiveness evaluation – How well managers support, develop and retain their staff.
- High-performer retention – Whether the organization keeps its best performers over time.
- HR staff-to-employee ratio/HR cost per FTE – How efficiently the HR function is structured relative to the wider workforce.
- Manager-to-employee ratio/leverage analysis – The span of control managers have, and whether it supports or hinders team performance.
- Workforce/seniority pyramid – Visualizes the distribution of junior, mid-level and senior staff to ensure a healthy talent pipeline.
- Staff utilization rates – How effectively employees' time and skills are being used
- Workforce structure – How teams, functions and reporting lines are organized to support business goals.
- 9 Box analysis grid – A 3×3 grid that plots employees by performance and potential to identify future leaders, develop talent or plan succession.

SLICING AND DICING DATA

When you start working with people data, you will quickly realize that raw metrics only tell part of the story. What gives analysis real meaning is how you slice, dice and compare the numbers. Comparison is where insights start to emerge, and where you can make a real impact.[1] So, how should you slice your data to get most insights through comparison? There are three major ways: time, demographics and employment attributes.

- **Slicing by time** helps you spot trends and patterns over different periods. You might look at fields like tenure, cohort, month, quarter or year, or time to event.
- **Slicing by demographics** helps you explore how experiences differ between groups. Common cuts include: gender, ethnicity, age, nationality, generation, religion, special adjustments, neuro-diversity attributes. They can reveal important gaps in fairness and opportunity. These insights also feed into growing diversity and inclusion reporting needs.[2]
- **Slicing by employment attributes** lets you see how outcomes vary across different roles and work setups, such as: job level, department or function, skills, employment type (full-time, part-time, contractor), work mode (remote, hybrid, on-site), employment geographic location, internal versus external hire.

Slicing data by time, demographics and employment attributes turns simple reporting into powerful workforce insights which will convert into real credibility in PA.

TOP TIP
What are all these tools?

The number of tools used in PA can feel overwhelming at first: Excel, Power BI, Tableau, Qlik, R, Python, Orange and more. People love to label them as good or bad, advanced or basic. The truth is, they are more similar than different.

Almost every tool follows the same basic steps we covered in Chapter 7 – data integration, science, visualization and communication. The main ones you'll encounter are:

- Databases and data warehouses (like Microsoft SQL Server, Oracle Database, Amazon Redshift, Snowflake, Google BigQuery and Databricks) store structured data, pulling from systems like HRIS, finance and CRM platforms.

- Data Integration and ETL tools (like Microsoft Azure Data Factory, AWS Glue, Google Dataflow, Informatica) help move, transform and integrate data from multiple systems. Here, you can either use SQL to query the data or use no-code interfaces.

- Full Stack BI tools (Power BI with Power Query, Tableau with Tableau Prep, QlikView/Qlik Sense) give you powerful visualization and reporting with built-in data integration and cleaning features.

- Programming and analysis tools (Excel, Python, R, Orange) allow deeper custom modelling and automation but need more technical skills.

- Big data processing tools (Databricks, Hadoop, Apache Spark, Azure Synapse Analytics, Google BigQuery) allow large-scale transformation, analysis and machine learning across billions of records.

- Vendor platforms (like Visier, One Model) automate data connection, cleaning, reporting, modelling and visualization based on your specification and subscription.

Even though the interfaces differ, whether you add calculated columns in Excel, new steps in Power Query, drag-and-drop in Tableau Prep or code in Python, you are doing the same essential work: cleaning data, making sense of it, and telling a clear story.

A lot of people mistake Power BI and Tableau as data visualization tools only, vastly underestimating their value. When you get to know these tools and their full capabilities, you can pick the right tool for you and your audience.

You have probably noticed that there are several major cloud providers, Microsoft (Azure), Google (Google Cloud Platform GCP) and Amazon (Amazon Web Services); they all offer similar data capabilities, just under different product names. Regardless of the platform, the logic in product development generally follows the data analytics lifecycle.

Problems related to synthesis

Now let's move on to common problems that require synthesis to solve. Low disclosure rates or people withholding information about their identity, needs or experiences may signal that there are deeper organizational issues at play. These problems are not just data problems. They are system problems.

As a PA professional, you must accept that you will not always have the power to fix these problems yourself. Analytics alone cannot resolve broken processes, rebuild trust or reshape leadership culture. But you are responsible for recognizing these systemic issues, highlighting them clearly and calling them out. It requires knowledge, courage, clarity and a business-owner mindset.

Here are some common synthesis problems in PA that link to bigger organizational patterns.

DATA GOVERNANCE

According to IBM, data governance is the data management discipline that focuses on the quality, security and availability of an organization's data.[3] PA data governance links into the broader data governance processes across the entire organization. In some businesses, you might have a clear seat at the table; in others, governance will be led by data, legal or IT teams. You may or may not be responsible for running governance processes, but it is always good to know the common principles and language.

Common data governance keywords you should know:

- Data stewardship – who owns and maintains the data.
- Data retention – how long data should be stored.
- Access control – who can see or use certain types of data.
- Data lineage – where the data comes from and how it moves through systems.
- Master data management – keeping consistent and reliable core data.

- Data hygiene – keep data clean.
- Single source of truth – not having duplicated view of the same fields stored in different systems.

> **Common software used in data governance:** Collibra, Microsoft Purview, Informatica, SAP Data Services.

DATA LITERACY

The data literacy of your audience massively influences how seriously your insights will be taken.[4] If decision-makers cannot read or question the data properly, even the best analysis risks being misunderstood or ignored. Because of this, it is in your interest to support and build data literacy efforts across the organization. This can involve workshops, drop-in sessions or simple one-to-one conversations explaining what an analysis method means. Building data literacy is a hidden superpower. It makes your work land more effectively.

Key data literacy keywords you should know include:

- Data storytelling – turning analysis into a clear, compelling story.
- Confidence intervals – how much uncertainty there is around a number.
- Correlation versus causation – just because two things move together doesn't mean one causes the other.
- Analytics maturity – refer to Chapter 1.

EXTERNAL BENCHMARKING

External benchmarking[5] connects your internal data to the external environment, helping you move beyond isolated metrics. Sometimes, internal trends alone can't reveal whether a result is a genuine risk or just normal variation. Benchmarking answers critical questions like: Are we performing in line with industry norms? Are we investing at comparable levels to peers? Are we maintaining equity against market standards?

Just like reward benchmarking compares pay and benefits externally to ensure competitiveness and fairness, external workforce benchmarking compares organizational health, investment and outcomes. In both cases, the goal is to spot internal gaps, validate strengths and guide better decisions.

When you benchmark well, you're synthesizing internal and external insights to challenge assumptions, sharpen strategy and boost the credibility of your analysis.

Key benchmarking concepts you should know include:

- External benchmarking – Comparing your data to industry or peer standards.
- Internal benchmarking – Comparing current data to your own historic or team data.
- Peer group average – The typical performance of your selected comparison group (mean).
- First quartile (Q1) – The value at the 25th percentile (lower performers).
- Second quartile (median, Q2) – The 50th percentile, or the middle value of the group.
- Third quartile (Q3) – The 75th percentile (stronger performers just below best in class).
- Top quartile (Q4) – Top 25 per cent in a benchmark group.[6]
- Median benchmark – The middle value of a benchmark set, often more stable than the mean.
- Market reference point – A key external figure you measure yourself against.
- Relative positioning – Your standing versus the benchmark (e.g. above or below median).[7]
- Normalization – Adjusting for factors like size or location to ensure fair comparisons.
- Bell curve – informal term for normal distribution (covered in Chapter 7).

> **External benchmarking sources:** LinkedIn Talent Insights (workforce and skills across industries, companies and geography), Mercer Benchmark Databases, Gartner HR Benchmarks, Government benchmarks such as OECD, Office for National Statistics (UK), Bureau of Labor Statistics (US), salary benchmarking services such as Radford, Payscale.

AUTOMATION

Automation in PA usually involves automating routine data processes. Good automation frees up your time for deeper, more valuable work. The main areas you will see automation include:

- Data integration and ETL – moving and cleaning data from different systems.
- Analysis automation – pre-scheduled reports, alerts, dashboards refresh.
- Machine learning (ML) automation – Anomaly detection, natural language processing and clustering.
- Data access management (automatically controlling who can see what).
- Demand capture and process scheduling (automating how new analytics requests are logged and tracked).

Common automation keywords you should know:

- API – connecting different software systems.
- ETL pipelines (automating data movement).
- RPA (robotic process automation) – automating manual, repetitive tasks.
- Workflow orchestration – coordinating multiple processes automatically.
- ML pipelines: automating machine learning models from training to deployment.

> **Common software used for automation in analytics:** Microsoft Power Automate, UiPath, Alteryx.

> **For ML automation specifically:** Azure Machine Learning, Tensorflow, Google Vertex AI, Python, R.

EMPLOYEE ENGAGEMENT

When you are asked to analyse low engagement scores or poor employee experience, it can feel overwhelming at first. Nearly all engagement problems boil down to one or more of three systemic causes:

- Leadership – Are leaders trusted, inspiring and supportive?
- Culture – Is the environment inclusive, fair and empowering?
- Work – Is the actual day-to-day experience meaningful and manageable?

When stakeholders push you for reasons why engagement is low, thinking in these three buckets will rarely steer you wrong. Always start by asking: Is this a leadership issue, a culture issue, a work issue or a mix of all three?

> **Common software used for engagement analysis:** Glint (Microsoft), Qualtrics, Peakon (Workday), Culture Amp, Perceptyx, Medallia.

VENDOR MANAGEMENT

As PA grows, many organizations bring in external vendors for surveys, technology platforms, analytics tools and consultancy services. This introduces a new challenge: vendor management. You might not lead vendor contracts early in your career, but you will often work closely with vendors, especially if they provide platforms for engagement analysis, feedback, data automation or AI-based solutions. Understanding how to manage these relationships is critical for ensuring quality, value for money, and smooth integration with internal systems.

Key aspects of vendor management include:

- Vendor selection: Helping assess which external providers best fit the organization's needs (for example, comparing survey platforms or workforce planning tools).
- SLAs: Understanding what service guarantees the vendor has committed to, such as uptime, update frequencies and issue resolution times.
- Data privacy and security: Ensuring the vendor meets legal and internal standards for handling employee data, especially under GDPR, CCPA or ISO certifications.
- Integration with internal systems: Checking how easily external tools connect with HRIS, finance systems or internal analytics dashboards.
- Ongoing vendor review: Monitoring how well the vendor delivers value over time, including reliability, innovation and customer support responsiveness.
- Exit planning: Knowing how data will be handed back or deleted if the contract ends.
- If you work in PA, you will often play a key role in testing vendors' data models, validation methods or user interfaces, even if procurement owns the formal contract.

Common software vendors you might work with include:

- HRIS Vendors like SAP SuccessFactors, Workday, Oracle HCM Cloud, ADP, HiBob, Sage People.
- Engagement platforms like Glint, Qualtrics, Culture Amp, Perceptyx.
- Workforce planning platforms like eQ8, Orgvue, Reejig.
- People data integration and analytics platforms like One Model, Visier, SplashBI.

TOP TIP
The great PA tools debate

Spend any time around PA professionals and you will quickly hear debates about which tool is the 'best' for doing PA work. Some swear by advanced languages like Python or R. Others champion platforms like Power BI, Tableau or integrated HR analytics modules in systems like Workday or SuccessFactors. The best tool is not the flashiest or the most statistically sophisticated. The best tool is the one that works in your environment and drives adoption.

Highly sophisticated, statistics-backed retention models built in R, complete with multiple regression analysis types, predictive accuracy tests and polished reports might be too complex and intimidating for senior leaders. The results may never make it past their debut presentation, and the insight will be unused. In contrast, building a simple trend-based version in Excel that's easier to explain and interact with might be more likely to see findings adopted, funded and actioned.

What matters most is not whether the tool is 'technically impressive', but whether the audience can understand and trust the outputs, the insights can be acted on without a PhD in data science, and the solution fits into existing decision-making processes

In some organizations, an Excel-based dashboard with simple visuals and clear commentary will have more real-world impact than a complex machine learning model that nobody wants to question or use.[8] In others, particularly more data-mature environments, advanced predictive models in R, Python or cloud-based platforms like Databricks may become essential.

The value of people analytics comes from influencing decisions, not impressing technical experts.[9] Therefore, it is a good idea to always match your tool choice to your audience's data literacy, the culture of the business, and the speed needed to drive action. Start simple. Build credibility. Layer in complexity only when the business is ready for it.

WHAT WOULD YOU DO?
Number 17

Imagine you have used Excel to complete a piece of analysis. A stakeholder insists that Power BI is a better tool for completing this type of analysis.

- How would you approach this issue?
- What would you say to the stakeholder?

Managing difficult behaviours and conversations

In PA, success is not just about running good analysis. It is also about managing difficult questions, different personalities and competing priorities.

You will meet a wide range of stakeholders, and some of them will be difficult and pose challenges to you. The trick is to be ready. Below is a list of different types of difficult stakeholder behaviours in the format of common archetypes you will encounter. Each one lists some strategies on how to handle them, and keywords you can learn to help you communicate effectively.

Difficult stakeholder behaviours

THE STATS PHD

These stakeholders know their statistics and take every model and metric very seriously. They are quick to point to academic terms and spot flaws in sampling methods, significance tests and assumptions, sometimes missing the business purpose by focusing too much on academic rigour. While trying to manage these stakeholders, it's important not to disengage the others in the room with overly technical conversations.

How to work with them:

- Respect their expertise but steer conversations towards practical application.
- Prepare appendices and offer technical documentation separately where needed.
- Focus on what's 'good enough' to make robust, timely decisions. Better to be roughly right rather than precisely wrong.[10]
- Normalize uncertainty through highlighting that scientific understanding is continually evolving, no model or dataset is ever final. Discovery, refinement, and iteration are part of good analytics, not flaws to be eliminated.
- If technical debates arise, summarize complex discussions in plain language for the benefit of non-technical stakeholders in the room, ensuring everyone stays engaged.

Useful keywords:

- P-value, confidence intervals, R-squared, sample size, standard error, multicollinearity, regression assumptions, Simpson's paradox, normal distribution, skewness, robustness.

THE PERFECTIONIST

These stakeholders have a keen eye for detail, and can zoom in obsessively on minor, often irrelevant points. They may focus on typos, formatting inconsistencies or outlier exceptions during meetings, drawing attention away from the broader analysis, the business implications and the decisions that need to be made. If not managed carefully, they can derail conversations, dissolve trust, stall momentum and cause teams to lose sight of the bigger picture.

How to work with them:

- Acknowledge their eye for detail but firmly guide discussions back to strategic outcomes.

- Offer to capture minor points separately (such as in meeting notes or action lists) to avoid derailing the session.
- Use the language of materiality and value, highlight that not every small inconsistency will have a material impact on the overall direction.
- Frame conversations around shared objectives, find common ground and get them to agree on something, even if it is the weather.

Useful keywords:

- Pareto principle (80/20 rule), materiality threshold, 'fit for purpose', business impact focus, let's not boil the ocean, listing assumptions.

THE RELENTLESS TAKER

These stakeholders treat PA as an endless on-demand service. Every insight you deliver sparks more requests: deeper breakdowns, alternative scenarios, or endless 'what if' analyses. Their enthusiasm may seem positive at first, but unmanaged, it can overwhelm your capacity, scatter your efforts and diminish the overall business impact of the work. Root causes of this behaviour often include:

- Excess time or bandwidth: Stakeholders who are underutilized sometimes fill space by requesting more analysis simply to stay active or visible.
- Disengagement from core priorities: Without strong alignment to real business outcomes, they get stuck in exploratory or perfectionist cycles instead of focusing on decision-making.
- Lack of analytics capability: Some stakeholders simply don't know how to interpret or act on insights. Instead of owning decisions, they keep asking for 'more data', believing it will eventually deliver certainty.

Recognizing these root causes helps you manage the relationship constructively.

How to work with them:

- Set clear boundaries around what is in scope. You want to document deliverables early and visibly, and refer back to them when new requests arise. A service catalogue (introduced in Chapter 1) can be a great tool to do this.
- Prioritize based on business value, not creativity or volume. Continuously anchor work to strategic goals, not interesting side quests.
- Buffer your delivery timelines through building extra space into deadlines to absorb inevitable last-minute 'one more thing' requests without sacrificing core quality.
- Deliver on the agreed date. Don't deliver early as it often invites new rounds of non-essential rework. Sticking to timelines reduces unnecessary cycles.
- Support capability-building where appropriate. You can offer simple templates, training, or guidance so stakeholders can start answering small follow-up questions themselves rather than outsourcing everything back to you.

THE CHAMPION FOR DATA-DRIVEN DECISIONS

This stakeholder believes deeply in making decisions grounded in hard data. They expect clear, numeric answers, and often drive conversations towards KPIs, financial returns and measurable outcomes like return on investment (ROI). Their focus on evidence and accountability can sometimes create blind spots when situations require nuance beyond what's directly measurable.[11] In PA, not every important insight fits neatly into numbers. Some gaps in available data may reflect broader systemic issues, like unequal disclosure rates across different groups. For example, if voluntary self-identification on ethnicity or disability status is low, it doesn't mean the data isn't valuable; it may indicate deeper trust gaps, fear of stigma or past negative experiences that need addressing.

How to work with them:

- Appreciate their commitment to rigour and business impact as it aligns with making analytics meaningful.
- Highlight that data is a decision support tool, not a complete substitute for human judgement.
- Communicate limitations openly and early, explaining margins of error, assumptions and the role of expert interpretation.
- Educate gently that lack of disclosure or incomplete data is itself a meaningful insight, highlighting trust, psychological safety or systemic inequality issues that numbers alone can't capture.
- Link qualitative insights and systemic context to business priorities like risk management, culture health and long-term performance.

Useful keywords:

- Correlation versus causation, data completeness, margin of error, non-response bias, decision support, ROI versus ROE (return on expectations), measurement bias, voluntary disclosure, systemic inequality.

TOP TIP
Flip the script

When stakeholders challenge you on low disclosure rates, it's tempting to defend the data or take on the burden of 'fixing' it. Instead, flip the script – reposition disclosure as a leadership accountability issue, not a data collection failure. Explain that leaders have an important role in building trust and psychological safety so that people feel comfortable disclosing. This approach maintains the credibility of your analysis and moves the conversation to where it belongs – culture, leadership and ownership – not endless debates about technical completeness.

THE MIND CHANGER

These stakeholders are highly changeable and unpredictable. Their unpredictability is driven by a series of factors such as workload, thinking methods and shifting priorities due to exposure to innovation in the field. What was urgent last week is forgotten this week. New priorities appear mid-project without warning.

How to work with them:

- Clearly document agreed-upon deliverables and scope.
- Build formal checkpoints to review priorities.
- Don't take action until the same idea is raised the third time.
- Add buffer in delivery timelines for any potential changes.

Useful keywords to learn:

- Scope management, agile delivery, change control, prioritization matrix, SLA.

THE BIG PICTURE DREAMER

These stakeholders are excited about big picture trends, the future of work and technologies of the future, such as AI, LLMs or blockchain. They are very inspiring and can have great ideas, but sometimes their 'big picture thinking' can be at the expense of solving real business problems today.

How to manage:

- Respect and accept their ambition.
- Anchor discussions in current state needs and achievable steps.
- Highlight the real impact of not resolving the problem on people.
- Learn from their ideas and incorporate them into the long-term PA strategy.

Useful keywords to learn:

- Gartner's Hype Cycle, large language models (LLMs), proof of concept (PoC), skills-based organization, GenAI for HR, skills wallets, responsible AI, AI ethics, machine learning.

THE 'MY WAY OR THE HIGHWAY' COMMANDER

This stakeholder expects outcomes to align closely with their views. They tend to treat data as confirmation for what they already believe, rather than a neutral exploration of possibilities. Direct challenges often escalate conflict or create defensiveness. They value control, decisiveness and clear strategic alignment.

How to manage:

- Frame insights around their strategic goals.
- Ask more questions to gently guide thoughts.
- Create a gamified experience to level the playing field.
- Where possible, offer options rather than direct contradictions.

Useful keywords to learn:

- Anchoring, gamification, scenario planning, strategic alignment, stakeholder management, option framing, choice architecture, control points.

THE FRAGILE EGO

These stakeholders are easily unsettled by negative findings, even when results are presented neutrally and professionally. People issues revealed through analysis, such as turnover rates, low engagement scores, succession gaps or performance trends, can feel deeply personal to them. They may perceive data not as feedback on a system, but as a judgement on their leadership or credibility. As a result, conversations can quickly become defensive, emotional or derailed if not handled thoughtfully.

How to work with them:

- Use solution-oriented framing.
- Use a consultative approach to make them part of the insights generation, so the solution gives them a sense of ownership.
- Focus discussions on future-oriented topics rather than past-oriented topics.

- Frame the findings as stepping stones to success rather than evidence of incompetence, position insights as part of a natural growth journey, not proof of failure.
- Offer them a graceful exit from defensiveness by validating their intentions ('We know your team's working hard') while gently redirecting focus to external factors or systemic improvements. Avoid cornering them or forcing full acknowledgement of fault in public settings.

Useful keywords to learn:

- Action planning, growth mindset, positive framing, psychological safety, co-creation, design thinking, gamification.

THE ENTHUSIAST WHO DISAPPEARS

Some stakeholders are highly engaged at the beginning of a project; they offer ideas, set expectations and shape priorities, but then gradually (or suddenly) vanish when decisions, data inputs or approvals are needed most. They may stop attending meetings, delay sign-offs or ignore communications. Then, close to a deadline or key milestone, they reappear with urgent questions, new demands or requests for changes, putting pressure on the project team.

How to work with them:

- Keep a documented trail of decisions and milestones.
- Set up structured check-ins to maintain engagement.
- Be proactive in summarizing outstanding actions and circulating the actions.
- Escalate early and professionally through the governance chain.

Useful keywords to learn:

- Governance checkpoint, project milestone, escalation process, project accountability, decision log, project charter.

Challenging conversations

Difficult conversations are part of doing any role. In a PA role, when managing projects and sharing findings, you're influencing how people see problems and view their teams. Emotional responses are inevitable in some situations. And when conversations matter most, they often get hard.

Difficult conversations tend to emerge when stakes are high, perspectives differ, or the message touches on identity, credibility or control. Your job is not to control reactions, but to understand them. The way you respond will determine whether the conversation leads to progress or shuts down.[12]

Below are ten common dynamics that can make conversations difficult.

1. WHEN HAVING THE CONVERSATION FEELS LIKE LOSING CONTROL

Stakeholders may feel sidelined or exposed when new tools or transparency are introduced. They may question your methods or express doubt about the need for change. Beneath that, there may be a fear of losing influence over decisions they've long owned.

What you can do:

- Acknowledge their expertise and involve them in solution design.
- Reinforce their importance in the future state.
- Use the II framing: the change is Inevitable and Imminent.[13]

2. WHEN YOUR STAKEHOLDERS HAVE TOO MUCH TRAUMA FROM FAILED PAST ATTEMPTS

Some stakeholders may greet your project with cynicism or fatigue: 'We've done this before.' 'Nothing ever changes.' These reactions often come from experience, not negativity, because it is natural for people to protect themselves from disappointment.

What you can do:

- Name the history without defensiveness.
- Ask: 'If it worked this time, what would be different?' or 'If you had a magic wand…'
- Deliver quick, visible wins to rebuild belief.

3. WHEN THE STAKEHOLDER IS DISENGAGED

Sometimes it's not a difficult conversation, in fact it is disconnection. Apathy, delayed responses or silence may signal that the person doesn't see the relevance or no longer believes change is possible.

What you can do:

- Personalize the work: 'Here's how this connects to your world.'
- Use logic, credibility, emotion and relevance to persuade.
- Lower engagement barriers; celebrate even small responses.

4. WHEN THE MESSAGE FEELS LIKE A PERSONAL ATTACK

Before presenting findings, especially those related to leadership or team readiness, you may face anxiety or avoidance. The concern is around how it might reflect on the receivers.

What you can do:

- Be transparent about who will see what.
- Use inclusive language focused on patterns, not blame.
- Offer a private preview before broader circulation.

5. WHEN PEOPLE HAVE VARIED VIEWS ON WHAT'S GOOD FOR THE ORGANIZATION

Some people challenge your ideas not to resist, but to protect the culture. 'This feels too rigid.' 'That's not how we do things here.' These are values-based concerns, not personal attacks.

What you can do:

- Acknowledge their intent: 'You're trying to protect what works.'

- Separate facts from conclusions to explore the disagreement.
- Translate your approach into the cultural language they value (in the context of different cultures).

6. WHEN THERE'S TOO MUCH CHANGE, TOO FAST

Even supporters of your work can become uneasy when things shift quickly. They may ask basic questions repeatedly or delay a decision because they're overwhelmed with information.

What to do:

- Normalize discomfort and offer reassurance.
- Break the information into small, manageable chunks.
- Gamify the experience to make the knowledge easier to absorb.
- Create predictability through structured tools, language and timelines.

7. WHEN THE 'WHY' IS UNCLEAR

People may challenge the project itself: 'Why now?' 'Is this really necessary?' If the urgency and relevance aren't clear, they'll naturally focus elsewhere.

What to do:

- Show that the issue is Inevitable, Imminent, and personal to highlight the need.
- Provide clear data and tangible risks of inaction.
- Share external benchmarks to validate urgency.

8. WHEN THE 'HOW' IS CONFUSING OR CONTESTED

Stakeholders may agree with the issue but dislike the proposed method. 'Why are we using this tool?' 'That system feels clunky.' This is about process clarity and alignment, not resistance.

What to do:

- Share your rationale for the approach.
- Be honest about trade-offs and limitations.
- Provide a future iteration opening (e.g. this system is being continuously updated based on user feedback).

9. WHEN PEOPLE MISUNDERSTAND YOUR MESSAGE

At times, difficult conversations emerge from miscommunication. People may assume you're evaluating performance when you're actually planning for succession.

What to do:

- Ask: 'What's your current understanding of this work?'
- Gently clarify in plain language.
- Reinforce the message across formats – decks, FAQs, visuals.

10. WHEN THE ISSUE IS NOT ABOUT THE MESSAGE, IT'S ABOUT YOU

Sometimes, the difficulty comes from dynamics outside the project – interpersonal tension, past politics or lack of trust in the messenger. The content may be sound, but it won't be heard.

What to do:

- Stay professional and avoid personalizing the reaction.
- Offer to bring in a trusted third party if needed.
- Address relationship tension privately and respectfully.
- Shift delivery to another person if it helps the message land better.

Difficult conversations are not the exception in people analytics, they're a large part of the work. The data may be objective, but the dialogue is human. Your impact will come not just from what you present, but from how you handle the moments when things get tense, quiet or off-track.

When you stay calm under pressure, clarify meaning without judgement and invite others back into dialogue, you get to build trust. That's when you turn difficult conversations into defining conversations.

CHAPTER SUMMARY

- Analysis problems can be categorized around time, mobility and capability. Knowing how to break these down and how to slice your data by time, demographics or employment attributes is key to generating meaningful insights.

- Synthesis problems such as low disclosure, poor data quality or confusion about data ownership aren't just data issues, they're signals of larger systemic challenges.

- The tools you use (from Excel to PowerBI, Tableau or Python) matter less than your ability to communicate insights clearly, match tools to the audience, and drive action.

- Handling difficult stakeholders and conversations is part of the job. By understanding common behaviours and learning how to respond with empathy and structure, you increase your influence and turn tension into progress.

REVIEW QUESTIONS

1　What are some of the common analysis problems you might encounter?

2　What are some of the common synthesis problems you might encounter?

3　List three different types of difficult conversations.

4　List three difficult archetypes of stakeholders.

Endnotes

1　Few, S (2012) *Show Me the Numbers: Designing Tables and Graphs to Enlighten*, 2nd edn, Analytics Press

2 CIPD (2022) Inclusion at Work 2022: Findings from the Inclusion and Diversity Survey, Chartered Institute of Personnel and Development, www.cipd.org/globalassets/media/knowledge/knowledge-hub/reports/2022-pdfs/2022-inclusion-at-work-report.pdf (archived at https://perma.cc/25MH-QJP2)

3 IBM (2024) What Is Data Governance?, IBM, www.ibm.com/think/topics/data-governance (archived at https://perma.cc/4W32-4FTY)

4 Qlik (2025) Data Literacy: Why It Matters for Your Business, Qlik, https://www.qlik.com/us/data-literacy (archived at https://perma.cc/B2Y3-KZBT)

5 APQC (2019) What are the Four Types of Benchmarking?, APQC, www.apqc.org/blog/what-are-four-types-benchmarking (archived at https://perma.cc/Q8T6-AR8E)

6 Wikipedia (2024) Quartile, https://en.wikipedia.org/wiki/Quartile (archived at https://perma.cc/VYU9-Q45R)

7 ScienceDirect (2024) Relative Positioning, ScienceDirect Topics, www.sciencedirect.com/topics/computer-science/relative-positioning (archived at https://perma.cc/8LKS-XEBL)

8 SAVVI AI (2022) When to Use Excel vs When to Use Machine Learning, SAVVI AI, www.savviai.com/insights/when-to-use-excel-vs-when-to-use-ml (archived at https://perma.cc/4YAW-MK59)

9 Barth, J (2025) From Overwhelm to Clarity: Democratizing People Analytics for HR Leaders, HRE, https://hrexecutive.com/from-overwhelm-to-clarity-democratizing-people-analytics-for-hr-leaders (archived at https://perma.cc/DZ2K-695S)

10 Read, C (1898) *Logic: Deductive and Inductive*, Simpkin, Marshall, Hamilton, Kent & Co Ltd

11 Molina, J and Connolly, J (2023) A Modern Research Profession: Government Social Research, Evidence-Based Policymaking and Blind Spots in Contemporary Governance Research, *Contemporary Social Science*, 18(5), 674–85, https://www.tandfonline.com/doi/full/10.1080/21582041.2023.2221249 (archived at https://perma.cc/D49B-JUC7)

12 Patterson, K, Grenny, J, McMillan, R and Switzler, A (2012) *Crucial Conversations: Tools for Talking When Stakes Are High*, 2nd edn, McGraw-Hill

13 Kotter, J P (1996) *Leading Change*, Harvard Business School Press

Conclusion

PA is growing from a niche to becoming increasingly embedded in how organizations think, plan and grow. You are likely to witness a huge amount of change throughout your career. For this reason, this book has deliberately avoided focusing on hard-coded technical skills, because who knows if those same tools or platforms will still be relevant in two years?

Sometimes, overly specific knowledge or dense technical detail that lacks lasting context can hold you back. It can weigh you down, especially when what you really need is the agility to adapt and the clarity to focus on what truly matters.

And that is exactly why the journey you have taken through this book matters. You are not just learning PA as it exists today. You are preparing to thrive in a future shaped by forces that are only beginning to take hold.

As you work through this chapter, reflect on your current skills, identifying gaps so that you can future-proof yourself and be ready to adapt to whatever comes along.

LEARNING OBJECTIVES

By the end of this chapter, you will be able to:

- Review and reflect on your skills in the area of PA.
- Summarize how you can equip yourself to adapt to the changing world of PA.

- Identify areas for future learning.
- Develop an action plan for continuous professional development.

Reviewing your knowledge, skills and behaviour

It's important to recognize that the skills landscape is constantly evolving. Treat the knowledge in this book not as fixed doctrine, but as a foundation to build upon, something to question, apply and adapt. Some concepts will stand the test of time, while others will inevitably shift as technology and organizational priorities change. For that reason, this book focuses on foundational knowledge, which includes principles and practices in PA that are likely to remain relevant, regardless of how tools and trends evolve.

As you progress in your career, continue to revisit the different skills you developed throughout each chapter, from relationship building to change management and project management, from systems thinking, to PA techniques and branding.

EXERCISE
Use a mind map to apply systems thinking

One of the most effective ways to develop systems thinking is by visually connecting the dots between what you've learned. A mind map can help you do exactly that. Instead of reviewing each chapter in isolation, use a mind map to bring together the key ideas, concepts and skills across the book. This will help turn your learning into a cohesive and interconnected system.

Start by placing 'people analytics' at the centre of your map. From there, branch out to major themes such as systems thinking, stakeholder engagement, branding, data storytelling, project management and business context. For each of these, add sub-branches with relevant concepts, tools or techniques you've encountered in the chapters.

As you build the map, look for natural connections. How does stakeholder management relate to storytelling? Where does branding influence how people interpret analytics? How does change management depend on your ability to read the system you're operating in? This exercise encourages you to think holistically and helps reveal patterns and relationships that might not be obvious when reviewing each chapter on its own.

The goal is not to memorize every detail but to internalize how the parts fit together. Systems thinking is about recognizing relationships, flow and feedback, rather than isolated facts. Your mind map becomes a living document of your understanding and helps you reflect, connect and apply your knowledge more effectively in real-world situations.

By taking time to revisit and evolve your map as you progress, you will deepen your insight and develop the kind of strategic thinking that sets PA professionals apart.

The future of PA

Some trends take off and genuinely transform how we work. Others fall into dust like many before them. Remember the excitement around AI-driven CV screening tools that claimed to remove bias, but often ended up scaling it instead? And of course, there was the era of personality assessments, advertised as a shortcut to understanding people, until we realized they often added more noise than insight.

Let us consider some current trends with a healthy dose of scepticism:

1 Skills ecosystem: Skills were on everyone's agenda; the hope was that the acceleration of AI development could enable skills orchestration and optimization at speed and scale. And what links to skills is workforce planning, being able to

monitor and capture skills at speed and scale enables the possibility of micro and macro workforce planning.

2   AI co-pilots and agents: The hope is that AI systems do not just support us but become active co-pilots in decision-making and actively start to make decisions in the process flow.

3   Casualization: While casualization has been the trend for a while, we may see increases in traditional career ladders give way to project-based, flexible ways of working. People will move in and out of organizations more freely, often working with multiple employers at once in a fractional capacity.

So, how do you respond to these shifts when they happen? Over-preparation is often overrated, and agility is far too underrated. You do not need to be the first to jump on every trend, nor should you wait until change is forced upon you. The real skill lies in recognizing the right moment to engage, not too early when the dust hasn't settled, and not too late when you are playing catch-up.

You don't need to predict every trend or be the first to adopt a new tool; what you do need is the ability to respond with clarity and confidence when the moment is right. That means drawing on the full range of skills you have developed here.

This field will never stop evolving – and that is the point.

Before we wrap up, challenge your thinking one more time. Imagine a scenario. Five years from now, what if PA is no longer just about people? What if it becomes about human and machine collaboration, where success depends on understanding not only how individuals and teams operate, but how they interact with intelligent systems, virtual agents and algorithmic decision-makers?

Picture a workplace where every team includes not only people with diverse backgrounds and skills, but also AI co-pilots, robotic assistants and predictive models woven into daily workflows. In this world, your role might involve:

- Monitoring and improving the dynamics between humans and machines.
- Measuring how well they collaborate, identifying where trust breaks down, where the workload shifts and what hybrid performance looks like in practice.
- Creating dashboards that show not only employee engagement but also how effectively AI tools are supporting teams.
- Designing strategies that improve how people communicate not just with each other but also with the digital systems they rely on.
- Organizational design, advising on where people create the most value, where automation makes sense, and how to structure work in a way that plays to the strengths of both.

STOP AND THINK

How did it feel when you imagined this scenario? Did you find it exciting, daunting or any other emotion? How well-equipped do you feel to adapt to a hypothetical future such as this one?

Your job is not to chase every single trend. Your role is to evaluate them with curiosity and confidence. Use the synthesis and analysis frameworks you have learned in this book to break them down. Ask what problems they solve, where they fit and when they are worth your attention.

And do not feel self-conscious if you do not know all the technical details right away. You are not expected to. The truth is, when a trend is real, the signs will become unmistakable. It will move from noise to signal. It will show up in your stakeholder conversations, strategic planning and the questions your leaders begin to ask.

When that happens, you will be ready. You will have already thought about it. You will have a mental model to build on and a sense of what questions to explore. That is your knowledge edge.

This is the purpose of expanding your thinking. Not to be right about every future, but to be prepared for the ones that matter. Keep observing. Keep questioning. Keep creating new possibilities from the macro trends around you. The landscape will continue to shift. Some skills will fade, new ones will emerge, and the tools you master today might not even exist in a few years. That is not failure. That is simply the reality of working in a field that constantly evolves.

Action planning for continuous professional development (CPD)

CPD allows you to plan for your future learning and development, taking into account experiences, skills, knowledge and behaviour, with the ultimate aim of developing your professional PA practice. But as we've said, do not get caught up in the fine detail of skills that may soon disappear. Focus instead on understanding the systems, the patterns and, most importantly, the people behind the trends. Learn how work works. Learn how decisions are made. Learn how change happens. These are the foundations that will keep you adaptable, confident and ready for whatever comes next.

Focus on building an agile mindset, a set of adaptable practices and a framework you can return to no matter how the context changes. What you do need is:

- The curiosity to learn.
- The agility to adapt.
- The confidence in yourself and the limits of your knowledge.

Action plan

Creating an action plan for continuous learning can provide structure and clarity to your learning and personal development. It can help you identify goals, set timelines and break

TABLE 9.1   An action plan for continuous learning

What is your specific objective?	How will achieving this objective support your HR career or ambitions?	By when will you achieve this goal?	How will you know when you have been successful?	What resources do you need to achieve your objective?
I want to be able to manage senior stakeholders at ease.	It will build credibility, help me lead strategic initiatives and gain executive support for my career advancements.	Within the next six months.	My name will be mentioned in executive meetings, I will feel confident presenting to and influencing senior leaders, I will receive written testimonials.	A guide in the organization, a sponsor, feedback from trusted colleagues.
I want to deliver data-rich conversations while telling engaging stories.	It will enhance my impact or help me make a mark as a PA expert and ensure the right decisions are made to deliver long-term value.	Within the next nine months.	I will deliver a data-rich presentation which results in actual policy changes/new initiatives, stakeholders will come to me for more insights.	Storytelling techniques, visualization best practices, mentor to test ideas with, tools like Power BI or Excel, presentation tool like PowerPoint or Canva.

down what you want to learn into discrete, manageable steps. You can then easily track your progress.

Use your self-assessment reflections to help you, and the template provided to set yourself some learning goals. Aim to set yourself at least three objectives that can help to further your skills, knowledge or experience. Provide as much detail as possible when drafting your action plan and the specific goals within it. Table 9.1 shows an action plan with the first two rows completed as examples.

You are entering PA at a moment of incredible possibility. Organizations are hungry for guidance, insight and leadership – and you are more equipped than you think.

So go on – be the future of People Analytics.

Answers to 'What would you do?' exercises

This appendix gives suggested responses to the 'What would you do?' exercises included throughout this book. These exercises are designed to help you apply concepts in real-world scenarios and reflect on how you might approach practical challenges in a thoughtful, informed way.

Each answer offers an example of how a situation could be handled. They are not definitive solutions, but rather indicative responses meant to stimulate critical thinking and help you explore possible approaches.

You may find that your responses differ from the below; that's completely normal. Check out what's different and:

1 Identify any gaps in knowledge.
2 Identify what you did differently that others can learn from.

WHAT WOULD YOU DO? NUMBER 1

In this scenario, a hybrid project management approach is recommended to ensure delivery of the recruitment dashboard in time for the leadership offsite in six weeks. By blending Waterfall and Agile elements, this approach allows for structured planning while also being responsive to evolving stakeholder needs.

WHAT WOULD YOU DO? NUMBER 2

The detailed project management plan and which methodology each task draws from (Agile or Waterfall) could look like the below:

1 Planning and scoping phase:

   ○ Begin with a kickoff meeting involving all key stakeholders to align expectations and clarify objectives (Waterfall).

   ○ Facilitate a design thinking workshop to explore pain points and uncover initial requirements collaboratively (Agile).

   ○ Use the workshop outputs to capture technical requirements in a structured format (Waterfall).

   ○ Co-prioritize the requirements with stakeholders to focus delivery around what will add the most value within the time constraints (Agile).

   ○ Agree on a timeline for delivery and develop a project plan and risk register to manage delivery risks, including time and budget constraints (Waterfall).

   ○ Define the minimum viable product (MVP), which is a clear deliverable that can be achieved and demonstrated at the offsite (Agile).

2 Execution and delivery phase:

   ○ Manage delivery according to the high-level project timeline, using the risk register to monitor and mitigate threats such as scope creep, overtime and budget overruns (Waterfall).

   ○ Take an iterative approach: rather than waiting for completion of major milestones like data cleanup or dashboard development, begin sharing early versions of the product to get quick feedback (Agile).

   ○ Provide regular updates and demos to stakeholders, ensuring visibility and alignment as the product evolves (Agile).

- ○ Actively engage end users throughout development to keep them informed that the tool is coming and invite early input to refine its functionality (Agile).
- ○ Hold structured weekly check-ins with the project sponsor and key stakeholders to track progress and adjust course where needed, always working towards the critical milestone: delivery at the leadership offsite (Waterfall).
- ○ Maintain concise and compliant documentation, ensuring clarity on project status, actions, risks and responsibilities, in line with HR standards (Agile and Waterfall).

3 Output delivery and future iterations:

- ○ Deliver a simplified but high-fidelity version of the recruitment funnel dashboard at the offsite, showing meaningful progress and capability (Agile).
- ○ Capture feedback from leadership and be prepared to refine and iterate on the MVP in a follow-up phase that continues beyond the offsite (Agile).
- ○ This hybrid approach supports the structured discipline required to meet a tight timeline while maintaining the flexibility and stakeholder engagement necessary to ensure relevance and value in the final deliverable.

WHAT WOULD YOU DO? NUMBER 3

To apply ADKAR at Tamari Bank, you could:

- Start by building awareness by explaining why data literacy matters now, not just later.
- Then create desire by showing how data fluency reduces admin burden, improves credibility and gives HR a seat at the table.
- Next, you could deliver knowledge through practical training linked to real HR problems (e.g. using data to reduce queries).
- Provide ability via hands-on teaching, mentoring and peer learning.
- Finally, reinforce the change with recognition systems, internal stories and badges for completion.

WHAT WOULD YOU DO? NUMBER 4

We can use Kotter's model to structure a bank-wide movement. Begin by creating urgency through the internal survey results and framing data literacy as essential for HR to retain strategic relevance in an AI-driven environment. Establish a cross-functional guiding coalition with influential leaders from each HR area. Launch a vision around *data confidence*, not data perfection. Deliver early wins, such as a pilot group using data to solve a recruitment bottleneck and communicate results widely to build momentum. Anchor the success by integrating data literacy into onboarding, promotions and performance reviews.

WHAT WOULD YOU DO? NUMBER 5

You can use Lewin's model to manage emotional and psychological transitions during the change:

- Unfreeze by acknowledging fear through a group 'heart to heart' session – create open forums for HR staff to express anxiety or scepticism without judgement.
- Begin the change process by introducing safe, hands-on learning sessions where failure carries no stigma. Use peer stories to demonstrate relatability.
- Refreeze by building routines, such as 'data check-ins' during team meetings, and integrating small data tasks into weekly roles.

WHAT WOULD YOU DO? NUMBER 6

You can use the 7S model as a diagnostic tool to ensure Tamari's HR function is structurally and strategically ready for data literacy:

1 Ensure the strategy includes measurable capability goals.
2 Examine whether the structure supports distributed learning (e.g. local data leads).

3 Align systems so that data tools are accessible and user-friendly.
4 Embed shared values that promote insight and decision-making.
5 Ensure leaders' style promotes inquiry over hierarchy.
6 Map staff capabilities
7 Build a skills development plan that reaches across all HR sub-functions.

WHAT WOULD YOU DO? NUMBER 7

You can use GROW to structure a clear pathway to guide HR team members' transition towards data literacy:

- Goal: Create a future where HR professionals feel confident using data to make decisions, enhance talent processes and work alongside AI, not feel replaced by it. Set tangible learning goals (e.g. 100 per cent of staff complete a baseline training) and emotional ones (e.g. increase in confidence scores).
- Reality: Most HR staff are starting with low skill levels and high anxiety. Many see data as foreign or even threatening. Current systems are underutilized, and there's a gap between executive vision and everyday readiness.
- Options: Offer multiple paths forward – tiered learning programmes, peer mentoring, team-based learning challenges and regular support sessions. Involve staff in shaping what learning looks like. Explore both skill-building and mindset-shifting approaches.
- Way forward: Start small with a pilot group. Use quick wins to build momentum. Track progress not just through completion rates but also shifts in confidence and behaviour. Keep the process iterative, participative and transparent.

WHAT WOULD YOU DO? NUMBER 8

You can leverage lean thinking and continuous improvement methods through the following applications:

- Create a learning loop of small, evidence-based improvements.
- Use lean methods to pilot and iterate.
- Begin with a single team or process, e.g. TA and map current frustrations (data friction points).
- Introduce a small improvement (a dashboard, a report automation, a new workflow), measure results, gather feedback and refine.
- Use PDCA cycles to continuously evolve your programme based on what works on the ground.

WHAT WOULD YOU DO? NUMBER 9

Reflecting what you have heard can help people feel seen and move the group forward.

You could say: 'It sounds like this has surfaced some different priorities. There is concern that we didn't see this coming and tension around whether to focus on preparing future leaders or supporting current ones. Is that a fair summary?'

The CPO might then reply with something like, 'Yeah, you are right… I think for now we need to understand the risk in our pipeline.'

This is the kind of clarity that discovery conversations can bring. It's not about solving everything on the spot, but building trust and helping people hear each other.

WHAT WOULD YOU DO? NUMBER 10

In this case, a few assumptions seem to be driving the concern:

- Many senior leaders in Production and Sales joined around the same time and are now nearing retirement.
- There are not enough internal successors ready or close to ready.
- Those roles will still be needed, in their current form, when the time comes.

You could highlight these and ask if it would make sense to start with them, to get clear on what the actual risk looks like.

Stakeholders may want to consider whether the roles will be needed long term, but you need a starting point and something to base the analysis on. It provides clarity and structure, builds confidence and keeps the work focused.

WHAT WOULD YOU DO? NUMBER 11

You can split this into two MECE issues, where each issue represents mutually exclusive topics:

- Demand for leadership.
- Supply of leadership-ready talent.

Looking at risk through the demand versus supply lens will start to give your analysis structure. You can assess whether the organization is heading towards a shortfall, a surplus or a balanced pipeline. And you will be better prepared to explain not just if there's a problem, but where it's coming from.

You can use other MECE categories to solve the same problem as well. For example, if you used internal versus external, you could then divide the problem into two different aspects – internal pipeline strength and external pipeline dependence.

WHAT WOULD YOU DO? NUMBER 12

After sketching the structure on the virtual whiteboard, you explain, 'From what we discussed, I think the best way to understand the risk is by looking at both demand and supply. On the demand side, we can assume the overall number of leadership roles won't change dramatically. The real focus is understanding where those roles will open up by function, region and skill set. Then on the supply side, we can look at whether we have the right people to fill those roles and how recruitment, turnover and promotion affect that.'

This approach is likely to result in agreement. It will make you seem competent and will reassure the stakeholders that the problem is solvable.

WHAT WOULD YOU DO? NUMBER 13

Below is an example of how you could guide this conversation.

You could take a moment to check alignment: 'To confirm, I will explore both the demand and supply side of the leadership pipeline. On the demand side, I will look at how many roles are likely to become vacant, where they are concentrated and how critical they are. On the supply side, I will look at recruitment, turnover and promotion to assess how well we are positioned to fill them. Does that sound right?'

Once they have agreed to this, you could continue with an estimation of work 'I can pull together an initial view in about three weeks. A couple of things might affect that timeline.' You explain that some of the data is still managed manually. Sales leadership records, for instance, sit in spreadsheets owned by the OD team. Sakshi agrees to help compile a summary version.

You raise another question: 'Are we assuming the current leadership structure stays the same? Or are there changes we should factor in?' Meredith responds to say that discussions are ongoing, and to use the current structure for now, noting it as a working assumption. You respond. 'That works. I will flag it as a limitation in the analysis.'

As the meeting wraps up, you ask a final question, 'Would you prefer the output in a written report, a slide deck or something interactive?' After a quick back-and-forth, you agree slide deck would be the best.

Then agree how you'll keep them up to date. 'Great, thank you, I will book twice-weekly 15-minute check-in meetings to raise risks and questions, and you can extend the invite to the necessary team members who might get involved in the project. Are you comfortable with this?'

You now have scope, data, timeline, check-in frequency and format all agreed.

Later that day, you follow up with a short email confirming what will be explored based on the issue tree, the key inputs and owners, the three-week turnaround, that the output will be a slide deck and that the current structure will be used with limitations noted. You also outline a simple plan:

- Week 1 for data collection and integration.
- Week 2 for analysis.
- Week 3 for synthesis and building the deck.

To keep things moving, you set up two 15-minute check-ins per week with Sakshi and Meredith to flag blockers and share early findings.

WHAT WOULD YOU DO? NUMBER 14

You might use SQL to pull leadership development data from centralized databases, Power Query to clean spreadsheets from Production and Sales and perhaps explore API access to automatically pull in training data from the LMS. This is likely to involve fixing inconsistent job titles, filling missing fields and ensuring formats are consistent.

The transform stage will take the longest. You are likely to need to remove duplicates, clean names and change the data format. Documenting your changes is important, either in a changelog or through Power Query's built-in steps, to keep your work transparent and reusable.

The final step, load, is about setting things up for future use. That could be saving a cleaned file in a shared folder or refreshing a connection each quarter. The goal is to reduce manual work next time.

WHAT WOULD YOU DO? NUMBER 15

You want to ensure that fields are complete, job titles and region names are consistent, values are accurate based on HR feedback, and data reflects the latest update cycle. These checks help catch issues before they reach stakeholders.

WHAT WOULD YOU DO? NUMBER 16

- Situation: The organization has a history of leadership stability but 38 per cent of senior Production leaders are set to retire within three years.
- Complication: Many of these leaders have no successors.
- Question: What is the risk to the leadership pipeline, and how can we close the most urgent gaps? Answer: Focus succession and promotion on the three critical roles and use flexible solutions for the rest.

WHAT WOULD YOU DO? NUMBER 17

A possible approach could be to start with a quick internal stakeholder analysis to assess how critical the stakeholder is to the project. This helps determine how much time and energy to invest.

If the stakeholder is critical, you can engage them by asking open-ended questions like, 'What were you hoping Power BI would add?' or 'Are you looking for better visuals, automation or easier sharing?' Once you understand their goals, you can explain the rationale for using Excel, perhaps for its speed, ability to handle complex logic or flexibility, and gently highlight how Excel features like pivot tables and Power Query may already meet their needs.

If the stakeholder is not critical, you can acknowledge their input respectfully, briefly explain the decision to use Excel, and take the conversation offline to maintain focus on the main task.

You can say something like: 'That's a good question, Power BI has strong capabilities, especially for dashboards and automation. In this case, Excel enabled quick and detailed analysis with complex logic. But I'd love to understand your goals better, and if Power BI aligns more in future iterations, that can definitely be considered.'

Looking for another book?

Explore our award-winning
books from global business
experts in Human Resources,
Learning and Development

Scan the code to browse

www.koganpage.com/hr-learning-
development

Our Brand New HR Skills Series

All the knowledge and skills for your HR Career

EU Representative (GPSR)

Authorised Rep Compliance Ltd, Ground Floor, 71 Lower Baggot Street, Dublin, D02 P593, Ireland

www.arccompliance.com

www.ingramcontent.com/pod-product-compliance
Lightning Source LLC
Chambersburg PA
CBHW042042030925
32042CB00041B/860